The Origins of Vowel Systems

Bart de Boer

OXFORD

UNIVERSITY PRESS

OXFORD

UNIVERSITY PRESS

Great Clarendon Street, Oxford OX2 6DP

Oxford University Press is a department of the University of Oxford.
It furthers the University's objective of excellence in research, scholarship,
and education by publishing worldwide in

Oxford New York

Athens Auckland Bangkok Bogotá Buenos Aires Cape Town
Chennai Dar es Salaam Delhi Florence Hong Kong Istanbul Karachi
Kolkata Kuala Lumpur Madrid Melbourne Mexico City Mumbai Nairobi
Paris São Paulo Shanghai Singapore Taipei Tokyo Toronto Warsaw

and associated companies in Berlin Ibadan

Oxford is a registered trade mark of Oxford University Press
in the UK and in certain other countries

Published in the United States
by Oxford University Press Inc., New York

British Library Cataloguing in Publication Data

Data available

Library of Congress Cataloging in Publication Data

Data applied for

ISBN 0–19–829965–6
ISBN 0–19–829966–4 (Pbk.)

10 9 8 7 6 5 4 3 2 1

Typeset by Peter Kahrel
Printed in Great Britain
on acid-free paper by
Biddles Ltd.,
Guildford & King's Lynn

To my parents

Contents

Acknowledgements

It is always difficult to know exactly where the origins of a certain work lie. Was it in October 1995 in the Ardennes when Luc Steels explained his ideas about the origins of language and proposed that they could be applied to speech sounds as well, whereupon I remarked sceptically that this seemed infeasible? Until then I had been working on learning robots, and Luc was not aware that I knew a couple of things about phonology and phonetics as well. Or were the seeds of the work laid much earlier, in 1989, in Leiden when I was introduced to the Nepali language by George van Driem? For the first time in my life I was confronted with speech sounds that were really quite different from the ones that are used in the languages I knew. My knowledge of speech sounds was deepened in the course on articulatory phonetics given by Thomas Cook at Leiden University.

Perhaps the origins of the research must be sought even earlier, in 1985 when Paul Lemmers introduced me to the fascinating world of computers, with the Apple II and the ZX-spectrum. This made me decide to study computer science at Leiden University instead of physics. Here Ida Sprinkhuizen-Kuyper and Egbert Boers introduced me to the field of artificial intelligence (AI). I decided to write my Master's thesis on the subject of learning classifier systems. After finishing the thesis, I had some time available which I spent working on a project in Brussels at the AI laboratory of Luc Steels. This was in the summer of 1994. After this project I was invited to do my Ph.D. at the AI laboratory of the Vrije Universiteit Brussel, which eventually resulted in the thesis on which this book is based.

First and foremost I must thank Luc Steels for providing the idea, the supervision, and the research environment for the research I have done. The money for the project has come from the Belgian federal government FKFO project on emergent functionality (FKFO Contract No. G.0014.95), the UIAP 'Construct' project (No. 20), and from the GOA project of the Vrije Universiteit Brussel. The funding has enabled me to pursue my research undisturbed, a situation that is unfortunately becoming rarer and rarer with the ever-decreasing budgets for fundamental research.

The request to convert my Ph.D. thesis into a book for a new series on the evolution of language, then in the planning stage at Oxford University Press, reached me when I was doing four months of linguistic fieldwork in Okhaldhunga, Nepal. I would like to express my thanks to John Davey and Sarah Dobson, my editors at the Press. I also would like to thank the anonymous reviewers of my Ph.D. thesis, who provided me with a number of useful suggestions for improving it. Other improvements were made as a result of the meticulous review by Francesco Lacerda, Jean-Luc Schwartz, and Amanda Walley of a journal article based on the work. It goes without saying that views and opinions remain entirely my own, as well as such errors, inaccuracies, and downright stupidities as undoubtedly remain.

Next I must thank my friends and colleagues at the AI laboratory (in alphabetical order), Tony Belpaeme, Karina Bergen, Andreas Birk, Sabine Geldof, Petra Heidinga, Edwin de Jong, Holger Kenn, Joris van Looveren, Paul Vogt, and Thomas Walle, for providing the atmosphere for good research, for discussions, and for feedback on my work. I also must thank the people of Sony CSL in Paris, especially Frédéric Kaplan, Angus McIntyre, and Jelle Zuidema for scientific feedback and for giving me the opportunity to so some quiet work at their laboratory every once in a while. I also wish to thank Björn Lindblom and Christine Eriksdotter for giving me the opportunity to present my work for the first time to an audience of serious phoneticians at Stockholm University. Special thanks go to my friends Egbert Boers, Igor Boog, Petra Heidinga, Stephan de Roode, and Maurice ter Beek, and to my brother Martin de Boer, for discussion of my work and for metaphorically kicking my behind whenever I got stuck or was too lazy.

Of course, I thank my parents. They always stimulated me intellectually and gave me the opportunity to study at my ease so that I could broaden my education outside the narrow scope of my specialization, thus laying the foundations of this interdisciplinary work. This thesis owes as much to them as it owes to me.

Finally, I thank my girlfriend Cécile Dehopré, for supporting me, making me feel at home in Brussels, and for putting up with my absent-mindedness, my lack of attention to her, and all the evenings I was not available when I was working on my Ph.D. thesis or on the book.

List of Figures

Tables

1. Introduction

Language defines humanity. It is generally agreed that what distinguishes humans from other animals is their intelligence and their ability to talk. Intelligence, however, is often defined in terms of language. The well-known Turing test, designed by Alan Turing (Turing 1950) to decide whether a computer program is intelligent, is based on the computer's ability to use language. Ethnic identity is also often defined by language. In Tok Pisin, the lingua franca of Papua New Guinea, the word for referring to people of one's ethnic group is *wantok*, 'one talk', meaning the people that speak the same language. The Slavonic peoples refer to the German people as *nemec* (for example, Russian немец), 'those who cannot speak'. The ancient Greeks called the Persians (and probably all other peoples as well) βαρβαροι, 'barbarians', supposedly because all they heard when they heard the Persian language were unintelligible sounds: 'Barbarbar . . .'. Language is essential for humanity.

Human languages are extremely diverse. Today, some 6,000 languages are spoken around the world. Although many of these languages are obviously related to each other, and can be grouped into large language families, such as Indo-European, Tibeto-Burman, or Austronesian, the links between the language families are much more difficult to establish. It is possible to reconstruct relations between languages up to a depth of approximately 8,000 years with currently accepted scientific methods. Beyond this time span, so much information is lost that reconstruction becomes speculative. As *Homo sapiens* has existed for more than 200,000 years and has been spreading around the world for at least 100,000 years, current linguistic knowledge suggests that many human languages have to be considered as historically unrelated.

Nevertheless, unrelated languages can have similarities in all respects: in their sound systems, their syntax, their morphology, their colour terminology, and also, for example, in the way they change over time. The similarities that occur in many unrelated languages and that cannot be attributed to chance are called *universals*. Originally, a language universal denoted a property that all human languages possess, but as very few such properties can be found, the term is now used for properties that occur in many (but not necessarily all) human languages. Sometimes the term 'universal tendency' is used. The study of universals can teach us about what human language is, what its constraints are, and how it is linked to other cognitive capacities of the brain. It is also important to investigate what can cause these universals. Chance and historical or geographical relations must be ruled out. Possible explanations can then be based on properties of the human brain, the function of language, or on historical processes. An understanding of what language is and what factors shape it will aid our understanding of the origin of language.

The origins of language and its diversity have always been subjects of speculation. Traditionally, language fell within the domain of religion. Language was usually seen as a gift (and its diversity a damnation) of the gods. Since the Renaissance, scientists too have started speculating about the origins of language (see, for example, Rousseau reprinted 1986; Jespersen reprinted 1968). Most of the early speculation was rather impressionistic. More recently, with advances in archaeology, neurology, and linguistics, speculation on the origins of language has become more grounded in facts (see, for example, the contributions in Hurford *et al.* 1998).

This book contributes to the study of the origins of language by investigating universals of human vowel systems and explaining them as the result of functional pressures and the dynamics of a population of language users and learners. It will be shown that in such a situation, regularities and universal tendencies can emerge as the result of self-organization. It should be noted that the language users in this framework are already capable of producing, perceiving, and learning vowels in the same way as modern humans can. The theory that will be outlined in this book is therefore strictly speaking not about the *biological* evolution of language. Rather it proposes a different mechanism (self-organization in a population) for explaining universal properties of human languages. The implication for theories of the biological evolution of language is that all phenomena that can be explained by other mechanisms do not have to be explained as the result of biological evolution, thus making the explanation of the evolution of language easier.

The goals of the research described here were twofold: first to investigate what mechanisms might be necessary for explaining the universals of human vowel systems and secondly to investigate what the role of the population might be in the explanation of linguistic universals. The research was part of a Ph.D. project (de Boer 1999) in artificial intelligence, which was part of a larger research effort to investigate the origins of human intelligence (Steels 1999). One can divide artificial intelligence research into two kinds: one that is aimed at constructing more intelligent computer programs and another that is aimed at using computer models to understand human intelligence. The research described here is part of the latter. As has been pointed out above, language is generally considered to be an essential part of human intelligence, and therefore learning about the origins of language is of interest in order to learn about the origins of intelligence.

As the research was conducted in the tradition of artificial intelligence, it is characterized by strong emphasis on computer simulations. Generally, theories in artificial intelligence are not accepted unless they can be shown to work in a computer simulation. By contrast, in linguistics research, results from computer models are still sometimes regarded as uninteresting and irrelevant to the study of human language. Another goal of the research described in this book is therefore to show that computer models of language can give interesting and relevant results.

The text of this book is based in large part on the text of the Ph.D. thesis. However, as this text was originally aimed at computer scientists and researchers in the field of artificial intelligence, it has been adapted extensively to an audience that has less knowledge of computer modelling and programming. In order to retain the interdisciplinary nature of the work, linguistic, phonetic, and phonological jargon is kept to a minimum and such jargon as is used is explained where necessary. Such explanation might be tedious for readers with a more linguistic background, but I pray them to excuse me.

This book consists of seven chapters. Chapter 2 introduces the universal properties of human vowel systems and the explanations for these that have been put forward by researchers over the years. Chapter 2 also discusses some earlier computer models that were intended to explain the universals of vowel systems. This chapter explains how the theory and the simulations presented here address the drawbacks of the previous theories and models. Chapter 2 presents the linguistic background to the research discussed in this book.

Chapter 3 explains the phenomenon of self-organization that is found in many complex systems in nature, and argues that it is very likely that self-organization also plays a role in the origins and the history of human language. The chapter continues with an explanation of the theories of Steels (Steels 1997*b*, 1998*a*) on language as an open, complex, adaptive system and the mechanisms that might be responsible for its origins. Finally, there is a section on the implications of self-organization for the study of the evolution of language. Chapter 3 provides the necessary background for understanding the mechanisms that are used in the theory and the computer simulations.

Chapter 4 describes the computer simulations in sufficient detail for them to be reproduced. However, an attempt has been made to present the models in such a way that readers who do not know much about programming will also be able to grasp the essentials of the model. A basic understanding of this chapter is essential for appreciating the results presented in this book and how they have been achieved as well as for appreciating why computer simulations are of use.

Chapter 5 presents the results of the computer simulations. It is shown, first, that the computer simulations actually work, and then that the emerging vowel systems are close to optimal and far from being random. The implication of this finding is that what occurs in the simulations is significant. The chapter then presents a variation on the basic simulation, in which the populations of agents change and have an age structure. These variations illustrate two things: first, in a computer simulation, it is easy to make small changes in order to investigate phenomena that might be extremely hard to investigate in real languages. Secondly, the results of the simulation are robust: variations in the details of implementation do not change the qualitative outcome. Finally, the systems that emerge from the simulations are compared with human vowel systems and it is shown that the relative frequencies of the systems that emerge correspond remarkably well with those of the vowel systems found in human languages.

The next two chapters are of a more general nature and do not appear in the Ph.D. thesis on which this book is based. Chapter 6 presents a selection of other computer modelling work on the origins of language. The selection itself is not complete and is mostly drawn from work with which I am reasonably familiar. It is meant in part to illustrate the possibilities of computer modelling for the investigation of the origins of language and in part to make links between this research and the other modelling research that has been done over the last ten years or so. Considered in isolation, the research presented in this book could be viewed as an interesting phonetic curiosity, but it only becomes really interesting when viewed as part of a larger research effort.

Chapter 7 continues in the same vein, but is much more speculative, and looks at the possible implications of the results presented in this book. The first six chapters represent solid results, but in the seventh chapter I explore the possible links between self-organization in vowel systems and self-organization in other parts of language—links that are not, however, based on such results. The chapter first provides an overview of the results presented so far with their implications for universals of vowel systems. It continues by suggesting how the theoretical framework used in this book could be of use for other parts of language. It then explores how more complex sounds could be modelled in the same framework and refers briefly to existing research along these lines. Finally there is an investigation of a tentative link between complex speech sounds and syntax.

Although this book may be somewhat optimistic at times about the role self-organization plays and has played in the origin of language and the explanation of its universals, it is not my intention to propose that this mechanism can explain everything about language. Language in general and individual languages in particular are complex phenomena whose origins and history have been influenced by many different factors as well as random events. However, I wish to show that self-organization in a population, as a process separate from biological evolution or innately determined development, can explain properties of vowel systems in an elegant way and that it is probably useful as a way of looking at other aspects of language as well.

2. Universal Tendencies of Human Sound Systems

Most human languages use sound as their primary medium for conveying meaning. Only sign languages use vision, and although sign languages are as complex and interesting as spoken languages, this book will focus on the properties of speech sounds. There are different ways of studying the sounds used in human languages. The field of science that studies the physical properties is called *phonetics*. Phonetics is ideally concerned with properties of speech sounds that are objectively measurable. These properties can be either acoustic (studied in the subfield of acoustic phonetics) or articulatory (studied in the subfield of articulatory phonetics). In order to write down the sounds they observe, phoneticians use the International Phonetic Alphabet (IPA). To show that the symbols represent physically measurable signals or actions, they are always placed between square brackets [ ].

Phonetics is (ideally) not concerned with the function of sounds in a language. This is the concern of the field of phonology. Phonologists are interested in the way different sounds can distinguish meanings of words. The stream of speech sounds is usually analysed as consisting of a sequence of separate speech sounds that are called *phonemes*. Phonemes are defined as minimal speech sounds that can make a distinction in meaning. They are generally written with a subset of the IPA, but in order to show that they are not necessarily objectively measurable signals, they are written between slashes: / /. In standard English, for example, /ɛ/ and /æ/ are phonemes, because the words /bɛt/ 'bet' and /bæt/ 'bat' have different meanings. In Dutch or French, for example, these words would be indistinguishable, so these languages are analysed as having only one phoneme /ɛ/, although the pronunciation of this phoneme might be [ɛ] in some dialects and [æ] in others. In describing a language, one has first to make an inventory of which distinctions of sound make a distinction in meaning, that is, which phonemes the language uses. It is usually possible to derive a fairly unambiguous analysis of the set of phonemes of a language.

However, there are some complications. The most important one is that it is not easy to separate the actual physical speech signal into phonemes. This is because human articulators do not produce phonemes separately, but start to produce new phonemes when they have not yet completely finished producing the previous ones. This effect is called *co-articulation*. Co-articulation causes phonemes to be realized differently in different contexts. This is called allophonic variation. However, not all allophonic variation can be explained as the effect of co-articulation. For example, the fact that the phoneme /l/ in English is produced quite differently at the beginning of a word than at the end of a word cannot easily be explained by co-articulation effects. Rather this variation is something that must be learned by a speaker. This variation can assume rather extreme forms, especially in languages with small phoneme inventories. For example, in the language Rotokas, with an inventory of only 11 segments, the phoneme /ɾ/ has allophones [ɾ] (an alveolar tap, like a very short d, or a trilled r where the tongue trills only once), [n], [l], and [d], all of which are apparently in free variation (Firchow and Firchow 1969). Linguistics therefore makes a distinction between the abstract elements that can distinguish meanings of words, called phonemes, and their physical realization, which is called *phonetic* realization. In parts of this book, frequent reference will be made to the phoneme inventories of languages, but with no reference to their actual phonetic realizations. The reader should therefore be aware that in using these inventories of phonemes one should always ask, 'What about allophonic variation?'

The research described in this book is concerned with inventories of phonemes, but explains them in terms of their phonetic properties. It can therefore be considered to lie between phonetics and phonology.

2.1 Regularities of systems of speech sounds

The phoneme inventories of the world's languages show both remarkable diversity and remarkable regularities. In the $UPSID_{451}$, the UCLA Phonological Segment Inventory Database (Maddieson 1984, Maddieson and Precoda 1990) that contains the phoneme inventories of a representative sample of 451 of the world's languages, a total of 921 different segments occur. Of these, 652 are consonants, 180 are vowels, and 89 are diphthongs. Apparently the human vocal tract is capable of producing an amazing diversity of sounds. Still, any single language uses only a small subset of these possible sounds. In the UPSID$_{451}$, the smallest inventories are those of the East Papuan[1] language Rotokas (Firchow and Firchow 1969) and the South American language Múra-Pirahã (Everett 1982, Sheldon 1974), both with only 11 phonemes. The language with the largest inventory is the Khoisan language !Xũ (Snyman 1970) with 141 phonemes. The typical number of phonemes, according to Maddieson (1984), lies between 20 and 37.

The phonemes that a language uses are not chosen randomly from the possible sounds the human vocal tract can make. In fact, some sounds appear much more frequently than others. In the case of vowels, [i], [a], and [u] appear in 87 per cent, 87 per cent, and 82 per cent of the languages in UPSID$_{451}$, whereas the vowels [y], [œ], and [ɯ] appear in only 5 per cent, 2 per cent, and 9 per cent of the languages. This is also true for consonants. Some consonants, like [m] (94 per cent), [k] (89 per cent), or [j] (84 per cent), appear almost universally, while others, such as [ʀ] (1 per cent, occurring in certain dialects of Dutch, French, and German, for example), [ʃ'] (1 per cent, occurring in certain native American and Caucasian languages for example), or [ʔ] (1 per cent, occurring in certain Caucasian languages), appear very rarely. According to Lindblom and Maddieson (1988) the possible sounds of the world's languages can be divided into basic articulations, elaborated articulations, and complex articulations. Apparently languages with small inventories use basic articulations only, whereas larger inventories use elaborated and complex articulations.

Phoneme inventories tend to be symmetric. If, for example, a language has a front unrounded vowel of a certain height, such as [ɛ] (which occurs in 41 per cent of the languages in UPSID$_{451}$), it tends to have a corresponding back rounded vowel of the same height. In this case this would be [ɔ], which occurs in 36 per cent of all languages in the sample, but in 73 per cent of the languages that have [ɛ]. Symmetries can also be observed in the consonant inventories of languages. If a language has a voiced stop at a given place of articulation, for example a [d] (appearing in 27 per cent of the languages in UPSID$_{451}$), it usually also has the corresponding voiceless stop with the same place of articulation. In the example this is [t], which appears in 40 per cent of the languages of the sample, but in 83 per cent of the languages that have a [d]. In general, languages use the full range of possible combina-

---

[1] Details of genetic affiliation and location of languages have been taken from Grimes (1996).

tions of place of articulation and manner of articulation (voiced, voiceless, plosive, fricative, etc.) rather than a subset of these.

This implies that some systems of speech sounds will occur more frequently than others. In fact, this is even more strongly the case than would be predicted from the above-mentioned symmetries. In principle a three-vowel system consisting of [i], [a], and [u] would seem only slightly more likely than a system consisting of [ɛ], [a], and [ɔ] (if we consider the a priori probabilities of the different segments). However, in a previous version of the UPSID with 317 languages, the former system occurs ten times, while the latter system does not occur at all (Vallée 1994, Appendix 2). The most common vowel system is the one consisting of [i], [e], [a], [o], and [u]. This occurs in 34 of the 317 languages (Vallée 1994), much more often than any other system. Certain systems seem to be favoured, while others seem to be avoided.

2.2 Regularities of speech sound sequences

Further regularities can be found in the way languages combine sounds into syllables and words. The field that studies the way in which sounds can be combined into words is called *phonotactics*. A syllable is generally thought to consist of a nucleus that is preceded by an optional onset, and that is followed by an optional coda. For example, in the word 'small' the /a/ is the nucleus, /sm/ is the onset, and /l/ is the coda. There is a debate about the nature of the relationship between these three elements, but it is not important for the present discussion.

One of the most important findings is that all languages have syllables that consist either of a single vowel (V) or of a consonant followed by a vowel (CV). Syllables that end in a consonant (VC or CVC) are rarer. Also, in the babbling of infants it is found that syllables of the form CV are preferred to syllables of the form VC. Syllables with clusters of consonants (CCV, VCC, etc.) are rarer still. Complex codas are again rarer than complex onsets. In fact, the kind of complex consonant clusters that are found in Germanic languages such as English are actually quite rare cross-linguistically.

When a language has clusters of consonants, some of them are more frequent than others (Vennemann 1988). At the beginning of a syllable, for example, a cluster consisting of a plosive followed by a nasal, such as [gŋ], is much more common than a nasal followed by a plosive. At the end of a syllable, however, the reverse is true. The preferred sequence of the different types of consonants in a cluster can be described with what is called the sonority hierarchy. The hierarchy is based on the sonority of sounds, where vowels are said to be prototypically sonorous sounds, while voiceless plosives are prototypically unsonorous sounds. Syllables tend to start with relatively unsonorous sounds, will have a sonorous nucleus, and will end with relatively unsonorous sounds again.

However, a precise definition of sonority in physical terms is hard to give. It is sometimes approximated by acoustic energy, but the measured acoustic energy does not always correlate with perceived sonority. Be this as it may, an approximate hierarchy of sequence in syllables is as follows: voiceless stop ≤ voiceless fricative < voiced stop ≤ voiced fricative < nasal < semivowel. This hierarchy means that at the beginning of a syllable a sequence of voiceless stop followed by a semivowel (for example [pl], as in English 'please') is possible, but the inverse sequence [lp] (*'lpease') is not, whereas at the end of the syllable the reverse is more likely ('help' as opposed to *'hepl'). Note that the sonority hierarchy allows for syllables that do not have vowels as their nucleus.

This hierarchy not only describes the tendencies for syllables as they occur in human languages, but also helps to predict how words are divided into syllables by indicating which consonants will be analysed as belonging to the end of one syllable, and which consonants will be analysed as belonging to the beginning of the next.

2.3 Explanations of regularities based on features

The sound systems of languages appear to show great regularities. The traditional explanations of the origin of these regularities are based on innate properties of the human capacity for language. These explanations (see, for example, Jakobson and Halle 1956, Chomsky and Halle 1968) assume that there are (innate) features in the human brain that determine which distinctions between sounds can be learned. These features are usually binary. An example of a feature is nasality. A sound can be either nasal or not. Some of the features and some of their values are more marked than others. This means that certain distinctions are preferred to others, so that, for instance, a language would prefer to use the distinction high/low for vowels before it would use the distinction nasal/non-nasal. Non-marked values of the features are preferred to the marked ones. For example, nasality for vowels is considered to be marked. Nasal vowels will thus be rarer than non-nasal ones. In general, sounds with unmarked features and unmarked values for these features will be more frequent than ones with marked features and values.

Although the theory of distinctive features is quite useful as a tool for describing sound systems of languages, it does not work very well for explaining the observed patterns. First of all, it is not at all clear which features should be used or even how many features there are. There are many ways in which languages can make phoneme distinctions (Ladefoged and Maddieson 1996). Some of these distinctions are used in very few languages. Furthermore, languages make subtle differences in sound that are not used to distinguish meanings. For example, the English word 'coo', the French word 'cou' (neck), the German word 'kuh' (cow), and the Dutch word 'koe' (cow) are all pronounced differently and perceived as recognizably different by speakers. It is not clear, however, how these subtle differences would have to be represented or explained in a framework of distinctive features. Also, there is no clear hierarchy of markedness. This can be seen from the fact that phoneme inventories of languages can differ in one segment. If there were an unambiguous hierarchy of markedness, languages with the same number of phonemes would need to have the same phoneme inventories. Apparently the markedness of the features cannot predict the sequence in which phoneme inventories grow. Furthermore, it remains to be explained why and how these particular features became innate, preferably in an evolutionary framework. Finally, features and their markedness are derived from observation of linguistic data. There is therefore a risk of circularity in explaining the linguistic data in terms of innate features and markedness, which have been derived from the very same data. Rather, one would like to have a theory that is based on independent, preferably physical, physiological, or psychological data (see Lindblom *et al.* 1984, Lindblom unpublished).

Several attempts have been made to build a theory that explains the structure of human sound systems based on physical and psychological properties of human speech production and perception. The work of three researchers, Kenneth Stevens, René Carré, and Björn Lindblom, will now briefly be discussed. They have proposed different independent factors for predicting the sound systems of human languages.

2.4 Stevens's quantal theory of speech

Stevens's *quantal theory of speech* (Stevens 1972, Stevens 1989) is based on the observation that for certain positions of the articulators, a small change in position results in a small change in acoustic perception, while for other positions, an equally small change of articulator position results in a much larger change in acoustic perception. Thus the space of possible articulations can be divided into plateaux of relative stability and regions of rapid transition. According to Stevens, distinctive features can be predicted, or at least explained, from the positions of the plateaux and transitions. The two plateaux of stability correspond to the two values of the distinctive feature, while the transition region is avoided. The continuous space of possible articulations is thus divided into discrete, so-called *quantal* states.

The quantal theory of speech does not predict which vowels and which consonants will appear in systems of speech sounds of a given size. It is, rather, a theory of distinctive features. It explains from independent physical, physiological, and psychological arguments why certain distinctive features are expected in natural languages. It does not explain in which sequence these distinctive features will appear, nor does it explain why certain features would be more marked than others. Another problem is that some articulator positions are quantal relative to movements in one articulatory dimension, but not relative to an independent other dimension. Quantal theory does not explain why certain articulatory and acoustic dimensions are preferred to others. Although the theory is incomplete in certain respects, it does provide an independent explanation for the distinctive features one finds in human languages.

2.5 The distinctive region model

Another theory for explaining the structure of sound systems is the *distinctive region model* (Carré 1994, Carré 1996, Carré and Mrayati 1995). This theory considers human speech communication as a near-optimal solution to the physical problem of producing communication over an acoustic channel using an acoustic tube that can be deformed. The theory assumes that an optimal communication system can produce maximal acoustic differences with minimal articulatory movements. Minimal articulatory movements are defined as linear and orthogonal deformations of a uniform acoustic tube. A computational model is used with which the deformations of the uniform tube are calculated that result in maximal acoustic distinctions. This model finds deformations that result in an acoustic space that corresponds to the vowel space of human sound systems. The uniform tube is divided into four *distinctive regions* that correspond to the regions of the vocal tract that are used in vowel production. The model can be extended to predicting places of articulation of consonants by looking at maximal changes in frequencies of formants. The uniform tube is then divided into eight distinctive regions, each corresponding to different places of articulation for consonants.

This model is able to predict the possible places of articulation, as well as the available vowel space, from purely physical principles and from the assumption that speech communication is a near-optimal solution to the problem of communicating with acoustic signals produced by a deformable acoustic tube. However, this model does not directly predict which of the possible articulations will be chosen for building a sound system (although see Carré 1996). Note also that there seems to be a discrepancy between Stevens's theory and the distinctive region model. Given a certain articulatory movement, Stevens seems to favour minimum acoustic change whereas the distinctive region model seems to favour maximal acoustic change.

2.6 Predicting sound systems as a whole

Lindblom and Engstrand (1989) have pointed out (in a reaction to the quantal theory of speech, but their comments hold equally well for the distinctive region model) that for explaining the sound systems one finds in human languages, one should not look at the qualities of individual sounds and features alone. Rather, one should look at the role of each sound in the sound system as a whole: it should be sufficiently distinct from all the other sounds in the sound system. A sound might have very salient acoustic properties, but if the sound system already contains a sound very much resembling it, the sound is not going to be a very good candidate for extending the sound system. If one wants to explain the sound systems of the world's languages one should therefore look at systems as a whole, rather than at the merits of individual speech sounds.

A first attempt to predict sound systems as a whole, which does not consider the qualities of the sounds that make up the system, was undertaken by Liljencrants and Lindblom (1972). They predicted vowel systems with a given number of vowels by minimizing an energy function of the total system. The energy function is defined as:

$$E = \sum_{i=1}^{n-1} \sum_{j=0}^{i-1} \frac{1}{r_{ij}^2} \tag{2.1}$$

where E is the energy, n the number of vowels, and r_{ij} the perceptual distance between vowels i and j. The function adds the inverse square of all the distances between all the vowels in the system. In physical terms this corresponds roughly to the (potential) energy of a group of n repelling magnets. It is highest when the magnets are close together, and becomes less when they are dispersed.

The minimization procedure effectively spreads the vowels as evenly as possible over the available vowel space. The procedure starts with a predefined number of vowels scattered randomly near the centre of the available acoustic space. It then makes modifications to the positions of the vowels (within an acoustic space that is limited by what can be produced by the human vocal tract) and checks whether the energy function becomes less. If it does, the new state is kept and the procedure is repeated until the energy cannot be lowered any further. This procedure amounts to the vowels repelling each other within the limited acoustic space. It can also be modelled, as Liljencrants and Lindblom (1972) point out, by the use of repelling magnets floating in water in a basin of the required shape.

The simulation of systems with limited numbers of vowels produced realistic results. The systems that were generated correspond with the vowel systems that are frequently found in the world's languages. With improved methods of calculating the perceptual distances between different vowels (Crothers 1978, Lindblom 1986, Vallée 1994, Schwartz, Boë, Vallée, and Abry 1997*b*), the predictions made by the optimization correspond even more closely with the observations of real languages.

The same method can be applied for predicting systems of consonants, although it is much more difficult to build computer simulations of these. Work has been done on predicting repertoires of consonant–vowel syllables (Lindblom *et al.* 1984). Here the criterion of minimal articulatory complexity has to be added. In the sound systems of human languages one can observe that not only acoustical distinctiveness is maximized, but also economy of articulatory movements. If making sounds more distinctive requires much more complex articulations, it is preferable to use less distinctive, but less complex sounds. As Maddieson (1984, section 1.5) observed, the most frequent vowel system is /i, e, a, o, u/, not /i, ẽ, a̠, o̠, uˤ/. The latter is more distinctive acoustically, but much more complex articulatorily. A repertoire of basic articulations is used first, and only when the number of segments in the sound system becomes large will more complex (and more acoustically distinctive) articulations be used (Lindblom and Maddieson 1988). Of course, their use introduces many more parameters in a computer simulation, and thus makes them much harder, as well as more controversial, to build.

The point remains that sound systems of languages can be considered as the result of an optimization of the acoustic distinctiveness and articulatory ease of a complete system of sounds. The available articulatory gestures, the acoustic distinctiveness as well as the articulatory ease of sounds relative to the other sounds, can be determined by (among others) the models of Stevens and Carré. This optimization provides a fairly detailed account of *why* human sound systems are the way they are.

2.7 How sound systems have become optimized

However, this account is not quite complete. It appears that there are more or less optimized sound systems in human languages, but it is not clear *how* they have become optimized. Clearly, the individual language users and language learners do not carry out an explicit optimization. On the contrary, they try to imitate their parents and peers as accurately as possible. The nature of this imitation can be seen from the fact that people make and observe much finer distinctions in their sound systems than are necessary for successful communication. This makes it possible for speakers of slightly different dialects of a language to understand each other perfectly, but still perceive that the other speaks a different dialect.

The question why this is the case falls outside the scope of this book, but will be accepted as a given.

It appears that the sound system of a language is optimized to a certain extent, even though the language users and language learners themselves do not carry out any explicit optimization. However, there are individual variations in a language that tend towards ease of production, understanding, and learning. Apparently, then, there is a global optimization in the language, due to local interactions. This is an example of self-organization, which will be described in more detail in the next chapter. In order to investigate this phenomenon and to check how it explains the structure of sound systems, one has to abandon the point of view of language as a purely individual behaviour and see language as a collective, complex, dynamic behaviour. Owing to the complexity of self-organizing phenomena, the best way to investigate them is by computer simulations.

2.8 Glotin's AGORA model

Probably the first model that used a simulation of a population in order to explain the properties of vowel systems was the AGORA model of Hervé Glotin (Glotin 1995, Glotin and Laboissière 1996, Berrah *et al.* 1996). It is based on a community of talking 'robots' called *carl*s (Cerveau Analytique de Recherche en Linguistique/Co-operative Agent for Research in Linguistics). Each *carl* has a repertoire of vowels, and these are represented both articulatorily and acoustically. It is equipped with an articulatory model, based on Maeda's model (Maeda 1989), with which it can produce acoustic signals consisting of formant patterns. Initially, for each *carl* a fixed number of vowels is chosen at random near the position of the neutral vowel. In the simulations, two *carl*s are selected from the population at random, and they both produce a vowel that is randomly chosen from their repertoire. They then find the vowel in their repertoire that is closest to the sound they hear. They shift this vowel, so that its acoustic signal will be closer to the sound they heard, and shift all the other vowels in their repertoire away from this signal.

Depending on the amount of shifting a *carl* does, a measure of fitness is calculated. The less shifting a *carl* does, and thus the more it conforms to the sound systems in the other *carl*s, the fitter it will be. After a number of interactions between *carl*s, the least fit *carl*s are removed from the populations, and the fittest are used to calculate a replacing *carl*, by means of a genetic algorithm (for an introduction, see Goldberg 1998). The vowel systems of the replacing *carls* are initialized with a cross between the vowel systems of the parent *carls*.

After a while the population usually converges to a common vowel system that looks like the most common vowel system in the languages of the world for the given number of vowels (usually four or five). However, convergence is not guaranteed.

There are a number of disadvantages to the AGORA model. The first is that, owing to the complexity of the Maeda articulatory model, the simulations are very calculation-intensive. This made it impossible to use populations of any realistic size. The population size in most of Glotin's experiments was limited to five *carls* only. Also the number of vowels was limited to four or five. Furthermore, the model had great difficulties in getting the populations to converge. The genetic component was added in order to get more rapid convergence. However, this genetic component confuses the simulation (is the driving force evolution or self-organization?) and makes it quite unrealistic. It appears that a new *carl* can inherit a sound system, something which obviously does not happen in humans. Glotin is aware that this is unrealistic (Glotin, pers. comm.) but considers it a simplification of the process whereby humans learn the sound system of their parents. He says that it does not influence the outcome of the experiments much, except to make them converge more rapidly. Another problem with his model is that the agents push the vowels in their vowel systems away from each other. This makes the model equivalent to Liljencrants and Lindblom's (1972) original simulation. As the agents conduct a local optimization of their vowel systems, the interactions between them are not crucial for the shape of the emerging vowel systems. An agent talking to itself would get the same results.

2.9 Berrah's ESPECE model

Similar criticisms apply to the work of Berrah (Berrah 1998, Berrah and Laboissière 1999), which is a continuation of the work of Glotin. Berrah's model, called ESPECE (or SPECIES in English publications), is a simplified version of Glotin's model. The agents' vowels are now represented only in the acoustic domain, and the 'genetic' component has been made much simpler. This speeds up the simulation and makes its behaviour more transparent, so that more varied experiments, with larger populations and larger vowel inventories, could be done. Berrah describes a large number of experiments with many different parameter settings. The vowel systems that appear in the population of agents correspond very closely to the most frequent vowel systems found in the languages of the world. In the second part of his thesis, Berrah explores the effects of the maximum use of available distinctive features (MUAF) principle. He shows that by using a slightly different measure of distance, one can predict the phenomenon that available distinctions are used maximally before other distinctions will be used. For example, with vowels, extra features such as length or nasalization will only be used if there is already a minimum number of ordinary vowels. However, a discussion of these results falls outside the scope of this book.

The results of Berrah's experiments make it quite clear that in his model, too, the shape of the vowel systems is determined by the repulsion between the vowels of an individual agent, not by the interactions between the agents. He describes an experiment with a single agent that results in the same optimal vowel system as the ones with multiple agents (Berrah 1998, p. 72). Berrah's model is essentially the same as the Liljencrants–Lindblom model. Berrah realizes this himself: 'Remarquons, finalement, que le cas extrême où la société n'est composée que d'un seul agent revient, en réalité, à effectuer uniquement des répulsions. Par conséquent, le principe simulé dans ce cas n'est autre que le principe de dispersion globale.'[2] (Berrah 1998, p. 72). Neither Glotin's nor Berrah's model, therefore, captures the essential contribution of self-organization, namely: global optimization without local optimization. The optimization is still caused by local actions of the individual agents. The only effect of the interactions is that all agents end up with the same system, although this also has to be boosted by replacing non-conforming agents with copies of conforming agents.

2.10 How children learn

Although Liljencrants and Lindblom's (1972) experiments have shown that universals of small vowel systems can probably be explained as the result

---

[2] 'Let us note finally that the extreme case of a population that consists of a single agent boils down to performing repulsions only. Consequently, the principle that is simulated in this case is none other than the principle of global dispersion.'

of optimization of acoustic distinctiveness, more complex factors must determine the universals of larger vowel systems as well as systems of consonants and the way speech sounds are combined. A very important factor in this must be the way in which children acquire the sound system of their native language. If the hypothesis that self-organization determines universals of sound systems is valid, then whenever certain sounds or combinations of sounds are difficult for children to learn, they should be rare cross-linguistically. There should be an inversely proportional relation between difficulty of acquisition and frequency of occurrence cross-linguistically.

For this reason it is important to review how children acquire phonology. Although the simulations that are presented in this book use a learning mechanism that is admittedly unrealistic, some knowledge of acquisition is useful in order to be able to see where the simulations are unrealistic and how they could be improved for experiments with more realistic and complex utterances. The overview given here is based largely on the works of Vihman (see Vihman 1996). Another compilation of results on acquisition of speech is Jusczyk (1997). Special attention is given here to the acquisition of vowels.

The results of the research into the way in which children acquire speech sounds are not uncontroversial, and different sources do not always report compatible results. This has to do with the fact that conducting research with infants is difficult (in that they cannot speak to report their perceptions), and that research into the acquisition of speech sounds is a relatively young field, so that standard methodologies and research questions are still being developed. However, another important cause of the incompatibility of results is that research into the acquisition of speech is heavily influenced by the debate about how much of language is innate and how much of it is learned. I will therefore try to focus on results that can be observed directly, and will pay little attention to the theoretical interpretation of these results.

A first important observation about the acquisition of speech sounds is that it is accompanied by a simultaneous change in the anatomy of the infant's vocal tract. The vocal tracts of a human adult and a human infant differ not only considerably in size but also in shape. In a sense, the vocal tract of an infant resembles those of non-human primates more closely than that of human adults. There are four main differences, following Vihman (1996, p. 104). The first is that the larynx is much higher, so that the vocal tract is much shorter. This causes formant frequencies to be much higher, and the ratios between them to be different, so that an infant's vowels will sound quite different from those of an adult. The second difference is that the pharyngeal cavity (the throat, more or less) is much smaller. A third difference is that the tongue is much larger with respect to the vocal tract than in an adult. These factors, together, mean that there is less room for the tongue to move and make different vowel sounds. The fourth difference is a difference in the shape of the velum. This makes it more difficult for the infant to breath orally without also breathing nasally, which in turn makes it more difficult for the infant to produce clearly distinct vowels. During the first year of life the infant's vocal tract changes and becomes similar to the adult's vocal tract. The differences between the infant's vocal tract and the adult vocal tract raise the question of how infants can learn to imitate the articulations of adults, even though the acoustic signal produced by an infant for the same articulatory movement is quite different from the acoustic signal produced by an adult. This question is as yet unsolved.

A second important and well-documented observation is that the development of infant vocalization in the first year of life is similar for all infants and seems to follow a genetically specified trajectory. Although different researchers split the development into different stages, there seems to be a general consensus about what kinds of sounds are produced at what stage of development. The fact that the development is split into different stages is mainly due to the different criteria different researchers use for determining when one stage ends and another one starts. Of course it should be kept in mind that there is individual variation between infants as well.

Following the classification of Stark (1980, cited in Vihman 1996), the infant mostly produces reflexive sounds in the first two months of life. Such sounds are produced as by-products of non-speech activities, such as eating, breathing, and straining, or those such as crying, which express an emotional state. The infant also produces a number of sounds that are not purely reflexive. These sounds resemble nasalized vowels or syllabic nasals, and reflect the fact that its anatomy does not allow it to control either oral or nasal airflow very well. After this stage comes the stage of cooing and laughing, which lasts from two to four months. During this stage the infant produces fewer reflexive sounds and has more control over the sounds it produces non-reflexively. It is now able to produce more distinct vowel sounds and starts producing consonant-like sounds as well. However, the timing of the sounds is not yet like that in adult syllables. From four to seven months the infant is in the stage of vocal play. It starts making a large variety of different sounds, using both its vocal cords and different sources of noise. Voiced utterances start to have intonation contours. As for vowels, the infant starts to make these in the full range of different vowel qualities available to adults (although, because the infant's vocal tract is much smaller, their formant frequencies will be much higher). The child already combines sounds in babble-like syllables, but these are not yet produced with the regularity of real babbling. This starts from eight months of age. At first the infant will babble by repeating the same syllable over and over. This stage is called reduplicated or canonical babbling. Later, from about ten or eleven months, the infant will start to use different syllables in sequence. This stage is called the stage of variegated babbling. At approximately the same time, the infant will start using its first words.

The infant produces voiced utterances from the very start. However, these only start to sound like vowels from about two months. According to Buhr (1980, cited by Vihman 1996), children only start to produce a complete vowel triangle (delimited by [i], [a], and [u]) from about 24 weeks. This vowel triangle expands gradually over time. Kuhl and Meltzoff (1996) find similar results, although in their results the expansion seems to start earlier, at between 16 and 20 weeks. It appears that distinctions between [i], [ɛ], and [a] can be made first, as these involve only tongue height, which can be controlled by action of the jaw alone. Making a full vowel triangle also involves control of tongue position.

That the development of speech production is partly the result of genetically driven maturation processes is illustrated by the fact that deaf children also show the different stages in development described above. This means that the changes in behaviour referred to are not completely dependent on auditory feedback. However, deaf children tend to start babbling later, so there must be at least some influence from listening to their own production. Also, from at least the age of six months, hearing children show an influence on their production exerted by the language that is spoken around them. This influence has been observed, in particular, in intonation and vowel repertoires.

Infants' perception of speech sounds also changes rapidly during their early development. Of course, collecting data about development of perception in infants is much more difficult than collecting data about production. Infants cannot report about what they observe, so indirect observations need to be made. Ingenious experimental protocols have been designed that are usually based on the fact that infants tend to become bored by repeated similar stimuli, while they tend to react to stimuli they perceive as different. There is some evidence that infants are influenced by speech when they are still in the womb. Neonates tend to prefer the intonation patterns of their mother tongue, and have an even greater preference for their mother's voice.

As for phonological contrasts, it has been observed that very young infants are able to distinguish all the phonological contrasts used in human languages, independent of their mother tongue. However, when they have been exposed for some time to language input, they tend to lose the ability to perceive phonetic distinctions that are not used in their native language. According to Kuhl *et al.* (1992) an influence can be observed as early as six months. According to Grieser and Kuhl (1989) children eventually learn to perceive speech sounds in terms of prototypes (but see Frieda *et al.* (1999) for comments on this theory). One specific signal is perceived to be the best representation of a phoneme, while signals that lie around a prototype tend to be perceived as the same phoneme. It is much easier to make distinctions between signals belonging to two different phonemes than to make distinctions between two signals that belong to the same phoneme, even though acoustically the difference between each pair of stimuli might be the same. Untrained adults are generally not able to perceive phonetic distinctions that are not used in their native language.

How children learn the speech sounds of their language is still unknown. Parts of language development are clearly genetically determined, and parts are clearly learned, but for many aspects of the process it is not clear whether they are determined by innate factors, or whether they depend on learning. There is evidence, however, that there are also cultural adaptations that facilitate language learning. It appears that parents tend to adapt their style of speech when they address infants. Kuhl *et al.* (1997), for example, have found that in speech that is addressed to infants, parents tend to use more widely dispersed vowels than in speech addressed to adults. They show that this phenomenon occurs in English, Russian, and Swedish. This style of speaking is sometimes referred to as *motherese* or *parentese*, but it is one that seems to be adopted widely by adults when they are addressing anybody who might have difficulty in understanding.

Although the simulations described in this book do not use an accurate model of the process whereby infants learn speech, such a model should be used by later simulations of more complex speech signals. Also, computer models could provide insight into the learning process itself and into the emergence of behaviour adaptive to good language transfer, such as parentese.

3. Self-Organization

Self-organization, as the term is used in this book, is the emergence of order on a large scale in a system through interactions that are only on a local scale. Through its use by many different researchers in many different fields, and through the fact that there is no precise mathematical definition of the term, self-organization has become a rather ill-understood concept. The term (Nicolis and Prigogine 1977) might even have a slightly negative connotation for some researchers, not least because the notion of self-organization has been taken over by a number of followers of the New Age Movement (a book by the founder of the study of self-organization, Prigogine, and the philosopher Stengers (1988) has been published by a New Age publisher). That this has happened has to do with the fact that self-organization implies in a sense that 'the total is larger than the sum of its parts', but the New Age understanding of this concept is no more sophisticated than its understanding of the concept of particle–wave duality it has so eagerly adopted from quantum physics. In fact, self-organization is a phenomenon that occurs when a system's global behaviour depends not only on the behaviour of the constituent parts, but also on the interactions between these parts. Many natural systems are of this kind and in fact self-organization occurs in many different systems in nature.

In physics, an example is the regular convection cells that emerge in so-called Rayleigh–Bénard convection. In this type of convection, a thin layer of fluid is heated from below. As the hot liquid below is less dense than the colder liquid above, it starts to rise, but it is hampered by the viscosity of the fluid. If the temperature gradient is small, the fluid stays motionless, and heat is transferred through thermal conductance. Once the gradient becomes large enough, the fluid starts to move. However, the movement is not random; a number of regular cells appear, arranged in a hexagonal grid.

In chemistry there are autocatalytic reactions that turn periodic, such as the Belousov–Zhabotinski reaction (see Roux *et al.* 1983 for an investigation of its complex behaviour). An autocatalytic reaction is one in which the products of the reaction catalyse it, thus effectively amplifying it. In order for it to turn periodic, it has to be autocatalytic in both directions. The Belousov–Zhabotinski reaction is a reaction between a number of rather exotic chemicals that shows complex behaviour over time, starting from an initially homogeneous situation.

In biology there is self-organization in the formation of ant trails and in the building of the honeycomb. Ant trails are formed by ants searching for food. Whenever an ant finds food, it returns to its nest, leaving a trail of pheromones. Other ants are attracted by this trail of pheromones and will start to follow it back to the food source. As long as there is food, the trail will be made stronger. When the food is finished, returning ants will no longer leave pheromones, and the pheromones along the trail will eventually evaporate. In this way, ant trails emerge that follow near-optimal paths to the largest food sources. The honeycomb is another excellent illustration of self-organization: there is no centralized force that guides the bees to build a regular hexagonal structure. Instead, it is the local interactions between individual bees working near to each other, and all having the same size and force, that cause the almost perfectly regular hexagonal grid to emerge.

The examples of behaviour of social insects illustrate self-organization particularly well, because the individual interactions as well as the global behaviour can be easily imagined. They illustrate the importance of both individual behaviour and interactions between individuals. A single bee would not build a regular honeycomb structure, nor would a single ant cause optimal trails to emerge. Also, in neither case is there central control. The global behaviour is really emergent.

An important aspect of self-organization is that the number of states in which the system can exist becomes limited. In technical terms: the entropy of the system decreases. From the huge number of unordered states in which the system can potentially start, it evolves towards a much more limited number of ordered states. For example, instead of the huge number of ways in which cells can be spread randomly in a plane, in the honeycomb only a hexagonal grid appears. We know from the second law of thermodynamics that in a closed system entropy cannot decrease. This means that a natural self-organizing system dissipates energy. Of course, for computer simulations and self-organization in more abstract systems, such as language, this consideration is less important. What is important is that the system moves towards a state that is more ordered than would be expected if it were generated randomly.

In order for self-organization to take place there must be dynamics (the way the system changes over time) with positive feedback. Positive feedback causes a system that starts to move in a certain direction to continue to move in that direction. In the formation of ant trails, the positive feedback consists of ants depositing more and more pheromone, attracting more and more ants, who deposit more pheromone, etc. Often systems that have positive feedback will run out of control and do something dramatic, like explode. However, in self-organizing systems the dynamics and the positive feedback operate within bounds. In the example of ant trails, the amount of pheromone is limited because the pheromones evaporate and because there is a limit to the number of ants that can move across a given surface in a given period of time. Positive feedback in a bounded system takes that system towards a possible stable state, or *attractor*. In the simplest systems there is only one stable state. In more complex systems, there may be many stable states and surprises are possible. In fact, such a 'stable state' does not necessarily mean that the system is static; in the example of Rayleigh–Bénard convection, the fluid still moves, but the pattern of convection cells is more or less fixed. Through positive feedback, initial random fluctuations will be amplified and the system will always end up in one of the attractors.

It should be kept in mind that the long-term behaviour of a self-organizing system, as the term is used in this book, depends on two things: the random fluctuations in the initial condition of the system and the constraints of the dynamics. The reduction of possible states and the existence of attractors might seem to indicate that a self-organizing system will always evolve towards the same states, and that its behaviour cannot be interesting or will be trivially predictable. However, this is only true for the simplest possible systems. In fact, in realistic systems there are still a huge number of possible attractors, and these attractors can have unexpected properties as well. Furthermore, the evolution towards the attractors can be of interest. The possible final states of the system as well as the global properties of its evolution are determined by the constraints on the dynamics, but the actual attractor to which the system moves as well as the details of its evolution towards this attractor are determined by the initial conditions. Often the evolution of the system is sensitively dependent on its initial conditions. This means that initial conditions that seem to differ only insignificantly can still result in totally different behaviour over time.

Summarizing, self-organization as used in this book is the emergence of order on a global scale in a system where there are only local interactions. Local interactions are interactions between only a few individuals from the population at a time. Order means that the number of states in which the system can end up is much (by many orders of magnitude) lower than the total number of states of the system. Final states should therefore be unlike random states of the system. The system should evolve towards these final states in a way that depends on the initial state, but the final state should not necessarily be trivially predictable from the initial state. There should also be no hierarchical organization. Self-organization is caused by positive feedback loops in a bounded system.

Finally a caveat: the explanatory power of self-organization should not be exaggerated. Saying that something is the result of self-organization is not in itself an explanation. The dynamics of the underlying system should also be elucidated as well as the attractors towards which the system can evolve. However, once one has determined that the behaviour of a system is ruled by self-organization, it is no longer necessary to look for external causes of the organization, or to look for special behaviours in the individual constituents that would enable the global organization to emerge. In the case elaborated in this book, that of universals of human vowel systems, this means that all the universals that can be predicted as the result of self-organization do not have to be explained as the result of the evolution of the (innate, cognitive) human capacity for language.

3.1 Steels's work

The idea that self-organization plays an important role in language is almost as old as the idea of self-organization itself (Lindblom *et al.* 1984, Petitot-Cocorda 1985, Wildgen 1990). However, as has been pointed out before, self-organization is a complicated matter and theories about its role can best be investigated with computer models. Such work has become widespread in the 1990s since cheap and easy-to-use computing power has become widely available. In their work Lindblom *et al.* (1984) used a computer model, but not of a population.

This work has been influenced quite directly by Steels's modelling work on the origins of language (Steels 1995, 1997*b*, 1998*a*, 1999). Although others (see, for example, the contributions in Hurford *et al.* 1998, part III, as well as the work described in Chapter 6) are working in the same field, the influence of their work is not as direct as that of Steels. The focus of this section will therefore be on his work. But in order to understand his ideas, two more traditional views on language have to be taken into account.

Ferdinand de Saussure, in his *Cours de linguistique générale* (1915, reprinted 1987), stressed that there are two aspects of language: the imperfect language that individual speakers actually produce, with speech errors, reductions, interruptions, etc., and language as a convention in a population that is more abstract and idealized and of which all speakers know an imperfect version. He introduced the term *parole* for the first variety and the term *langue* for the second. He considered only the second form to be worthy of scientific study, thus effectively viewing language as a macroscopic, social phenomenon. Later linguists, most notably Noam Chomsky (1965, 1972, 1975, 1980), have taken a different view. Chomsky calls the speech that people actually produce *performance*, and supposes that underlying performance is a more abstract *competence*. Competence is the linguistic knowledge of an idealized individual in an idealized, homogeneous population. As the idealized population is homogeneous, it effectively asserts no influence on the individual language users. In Chomsky's view the fact that language is a social convention is therefore not relevant to its study. One could say that Chomsky views language at the microscopic level. The division of language into performance and competence is useful when one wants to write down the grammar of a language. However, if one wants to understand the actual dynamics of a language, including how it originated, how it is learned, and how it changes, this division turns out to be unnatural.

Steels returns to the view of language as a social system, but stresses that the *parole* or *performance* are as important in understanding language as the *langue*. The imperfect *parole* is the only kind of language people can observe and produce and is therefore a fundamental basis for the *langue*. Transfer of language from one individual to another is subject to noise and speech errors. Speakers have their own *idiolect*, or personal and incomplete knowledge of the language. Steels says that the macroscopic behaviour of language can be seen as the emergent outcome of the microscopic interactions between the speakers, just as the temperature and pressure of a gas can be seen as the macroscopic emergent result of the interactions between the individual molecules. Such a view incorporates diversity as an inherent property of language and allows us to consider language change and the language behaviour of individuals as two aspects of the same phenomenon.

A further element of Steels's view is that he does not regard the basis of grammar as innate. He admits that the language input that language learners receive is too little for purely inductive learning. However, he proposes more powerful selectionistic learning mechanisms that are able to learn quickly from limited stimuli. A detailed description of his learning mechanisms falls outside the scope of this book. However, if one does not accept that much of linguistic structure is innate, it remains to be explained why the world's languages show universal similarities. Although I do not want to take a position in the debate about whether language is mainly innate or mainly learned,[1] the work in this book will show that innate structures are not necessary for explaining (at least some) universal phonological properties of language. Self-organizing interactions in a population are sufficient to explain the emergence of structure.

3.2 Language as an open, complex dynamic system

In order to investigate language as a phenomenon of a population for understanding such things as the origins of language and language change, Steels has adapted the methodology and the terminology of the study of complex dynamic systems. Dynamic systems in mathematics are all those systems that change over time. Whenever such systems can be described in terms of linear equations (basically equations in which variables that describe the state of the system are only multiplied by constants or added to each other), their behaviour will be simple and predictable. However, most interesting dynamic systems are not linear and are therefore sometimes called complex dynamic systems, as their behaviour is not easily analysed or predicted.

In the context of language, the kinds of complex systems that are of interest are systems in which there is a large number of elements that interact only on a local scale in a non-linear and non-hierarchical way. This

---

[1] I admit that I think less of language as innately determined than is assumed in theories about universal grammar, and that the mechanisms that are innate are probably more general than what tends to be proposed in universal grammar. However, I am also convinced that one needs considerable innate, specialized machinery (both cognitive and mechanical) in order to learn and use something as complex and *large* as language.

means that the behaviour of the whole system is not predictable in any straightforward way. Most notably, as was pointed out in the previous section, such systems permit self-organization on a global scale without global interactions. This global organization is said to be *emergent*. An example of such a system is a colony of bees building a honeycomb, described above. A car is an example of a system that is not complex dynamic. It has many interacting parts, but they are organized in a hierarchical way. Iron filings following magnetic field lines are not a complex dynamic system either, as the magnet provides the non-local organizing force.

Language is a perfect example of a complex dynamic system, as defined above. The interacting elements are the individual language users. The local interactions consist of language users talking to each other and learning the language from each other. Of course such basic elements and interactions are much more complicated than in mathematical, physical, chemical, or even biological complex systems. However, this does not make it impossible or useless to view language in this way. If, for example, we can show that in models with simplified language users and interactions certain phenomena occur, we can be quite sure that similar phenomena will occur in language as well, as long as we have made justifiable simplifications.

In a language community, there is no central authority controlling the language. As the definition given in the previous section indicates, in such a system self-organization can occur. The fact, for example, that the language is and remains coherent is an emergent property and could be considered the result of self-organization. There can be other emergent properties in language as well, and this book investigates one of them: universal tendencies of human vowel systems.

Dynamic systems can be either closed (generally called autonomous in mathematics) or open. Closed systems do not interact with outside forces, while open systems do. Language, when viewed as a dynamic system, is an open system for two reasons. First of all, the population of language users is not static. Speakers can enter (be born or migrate into) and leave (die or migrate out of) a speech community. All of this can happen without there being any effect on the language. Therefore language is a robust system. Secondly, language is also an open system with respect to the things it can express. New words, expressions, and grammatical constructions can enter the language and be adapted by the speech community, and obsolete words, expressions, and constructions can disappear. That these happenings can occur has of course to do, in part, with the fact that language is used to talk about an outside world that is itself subject to change. In a sense, it can be said that language can adapt to the tasks for which it is used.

3.3 Language as an adaptive system

A system is adaptive if it can change itself (or its behaviour) in reaction to its environment in order to optimize certain internal criteria. Such change does not necessarily have to be explicit or voluntary. An animal that can change its behaviour in order to exploit a new food source and thus to improve its nutrition shows adaptive behaviour. A well-known example is that of certain birds that learn to open milk bottles. Adaptive behaviour is widespread among living organisms. However, more abstract systems can also be adaptive.

Language can be considered an adaptive system. It changes in order to optimize (implicitly) at least three criteria: communicative efficiency, communicative effectiveness, and ease of learning. Maximization of efficiency amounts to minimizing the amount of effort necessary to produce speech. This can be illustrated, for example, by the way in which frequently used words, such as pronouns, tend to be reduced, or by the way sounds and combinations of sounds that are difficult to pronounce (such as consonant clusters) are reduced. But the use of abbreviated versions of long but frequently used expressions is at the same time an optimization of communicative effectiveness.

Maximization of effectiveness is achieved by maximizing the success of the communication. Here the bottleneck is the listener, so communicative effectiveness can best be increased by facilitating understanding. This can be done, for example, by the use of a fixed word order for expressing grammatical roles if there is no case system, or by using fixed words and expressions for frequently used objects and situations. Such usages make it easier for the listener to predict what input is going to follow. Another way of increasing effectiveness is the use of redundancy: expressing the same thing more than once. Note that maximization of efficiency and effectiveness are to some extent in conflict. A compromise must therefore be found. The constant tug-of-war between efficiency and effectiveness also allows for constant language change.

Ease of learning is maximized by using as few items (words, sounds, and grammatical rules) as possible and by making the things that have to be learned as simple as possible, and at the same time as distinct from each other as possible. These processes can be illustrated by the loss of words for infrequently used cultural items or by the loss or reduction of complex case systems or verb paradigms (for a critical discussion of the role of these phenomena see, for example, Hopper and Traugott 1993). Optimization of ease of learning can increase both efficiency and effectiveness of communication.

In a sense, irregular inflections of verbs, for example, might seem to conflict with an optimization of ease of learning, but this actually depends on which is more difficult to learn: general rules or lists of words. It can be shown with computer models that in certain cases systems with exceptions can be easier to learn than systems without exceptions (Taatgen and Anderson, unpublished). But we do not yet know enough about how humans learn language to be able to decide this question.

No individual speaker, however, actively performs these optimizations. The global optimization must therefore be the result of local interactions. Optimization might be a result of the fact that language users can use different registers of speech. Speakers tend to have many of these registers. Some registers are more formal than others. In formal slow speech, speakers produce all aspects (sounds, words, grammatical structures) of their language to the fullest. In fast, informal speech, however, the utterances are reduced. As informal speech is more frequent than formal speech, children will tend to be exposed to this register more often than to other registers, and therefore might learn the informal variants before the formal ones (although there is a possibility that certain informal variations are harder to learn). The things that are easiest to learn and that are most frequent will be learned first. Therefore they will produce a slight tendency towards a reduced version of the language. On the other hand, things that are hard to learn or infrequent are most likely to be lost from the language.

New words and new fixed expressions can spread through the community of speakers by a process of *positive feedback*. In the example of a new cultural item, many new words or expressions will at first be created. However, some of these words or expressions will be used by larger groups of speakers than others. Speakers who employ the most frequently used words will have fewer problems in communication than ones who employ the less frequently used words. Speakers will therefore tend to switch from less frequently used words to more frequently used words, thus increasing their frequency even more and thus amplifying the process. Also, children will tend to learn the most frequently used words first. Frequently used words will therefore become more frequently used at the expense of the less frequently used words. This process will eventually lead to there being one dominant word, but of course new words may appear at any time.

3.4 Other mechanisms in the origins of language

According to Steels (1997*b*), self-organization plays an important role in explaining the emergence of and change in language. However, it is his view that other mechanisms also play a role. These mechanisms—which play a lesser role in the research described here—are *cultural evolution, co-evolution*, and *level formation*.

Evolution is a process in which optimization takes place by a process whereby the fittest individuals from a population are selected and less fit individuals are replaced by individuals that resemble the selected individuals. The best-known variant of this process is Darwinian or genetic evolution (Darwin 1859, reprinted 1985), the process by which biological species arise. For evolution to take place, three things are needed, apart from a population of individuals. The first is preservation of information from one generation of individuals to the next. The second is a selection criterion. The third is the introduction of variation. In genetic evolution, information is preserved by the DNA, selection is based on the fitness of an individual in its environment, and variation is introduced through mutation. In cultural evolution, the population undergoing evolution does not consist of biological individuals, but rather of ideas or knowledge, or memes as Richard Dawkins (1976) has called them. In fact, the cultural evolution of ideas might be Lamarckian (de Lamarck 1809) rather than Darwinian, in that ideas can be improved upon before being transferred to the next generation, while genes cannot be consciously improved. The power of cultural evolution can be illustrated by the example of writing.[2] Once writing was invented, human society was able to become much more complex, allowing for extreme specialization of activities. Also, dissemination of ideas became

---

[2] Learned and innate faculties cannot always be easily distinguished by means of research on brain functions. Writing and reading (which clearly are learned faculties) are excellent examples of this. There are brain lesions that affect only writing or reading, just as there are lesions that affect only speaking or understanding (see, for example, the entries on 'agraphia' and 'alexia' in Adelman 1987 and references therein).

much easier, thus making possible even more complex organization and faster development of science and technology, eventually culminating in the printing press, which accelerated the process even more...

In the case of language, that which is subject to selection is a person's knowledge of the language. Information is preserved as children learn the language from older speakers. Selection takes place on the basis of the criteria of communicative effectiveness, efficiency, and learnability. Variation is introduced through imperfect production and perception, but also by conscious innovation (for example, the invention of new words). Thus language is subject to cultural evolution. The fact that variation is not random, but might systematically prefer certain directions to others is not a problem, but might account for the universals found in language. Table 3.1 compares the essential elements in biological and language evolution.

Whenever multiple species evolve in the same environment, there is the possibility of co-evolution. A standard example of co-evolution in nature is that of the cheetah and the gazelle. The cheetah hunts the gazelle by trying to outrun it. This means that faster gazelles have a higher chance of surviving (and producing offspring) than slower ones. Over time gazelles will evolve towards running faster. However, faster cheetahs will be able to catch more gazelles, and therefore to raise more offspring. Cheetahs will thus become faster over time as well. Both species exert pressure on each other to become faster and faster. Co-evolution generally speeds up evolutionary change by increasing the pressure on species. Therefore it is sometimes called an 'evolutionary arms race'.

According to Steels, co-evolution can take place in language as well. In this case different parts of language (the sound system, the lexicon, the

TABLE 3.1. Comparison between essential factors in biological and language evolution

	Biosystems	Language
Information preservation	Copying of DNA	Imitation
Generation of variation	Mutation/ Recombination	Imperfect imitation/ Creation
Selection	Environmental pressure	Efficiency/effectiveness

grammar, etc.) are comparable to the different species. They exert pressure on each other, because they make use of each other. The lexicon uses the sound system in order to form words. The grammar uses the lexicon for words denoting grammatical function. The lexicon uses the grammar to determine which new words can be formed by combining elements from the lexicon. The sound system uses the grammar in order to determine which combinations of sounds are allowed, etc. Because all systems are separately subject to evolution, they will also co-evolve. According to Steels (Steels 1997*b*, Steels 1998*a*), this speeds up the emergence of complexity in the language.

The third mechanism that Steels proposes for the emergence of complexity in language is called level formation (for examples of level formation in evolution see Maynard Smith and Szathmary 1997). In level formation elements that are subject to evolution (and possibly co-evolution) join together in a bigger entity that then becomes subject to evolution as a whole. An example of this is the formation of multicellular organisms from single cells through a process whereby what were originally individual cells joined together in a larger organism that itself became subject to evolution. This evolution no longer takes place at the level of the individual cells, but at the higher level of the individual cells and their interactions that make up the behaviour of the larger organism, hence the name level formation.

Steels conjectures that in language, the combination of sounds into words, and of words into sentences, can be understood in terms of level formation. Both forms of combination have made it possible for more complex and more varied messages to be coded in speech. The process of level formation has to be understood if one wants to explain how grammar and phonemic coding emerged.

All these mechanisms work at the level of culture, that is, in terms of acquired characteristics. Of course, genetically determined factors are also important for understanding the evolution of language. It is usually assumed that genetic factors can influence what is learned, but that what is learned cannot influence the genes. After all, biological evolution is Darwinian, not Lamarckian. However, through the effect known as the Baldwin effect (Baldwin 1896), acquired behaviour can influence the genes. This happens whenever the acquisition of a certain behaviour confers a selective advantage. Genes that cause better acquisition of the behaviour then become advantageous, and part of the behaviour might become genetically determined. This effect is obviously important for language evolution as, for improvements in language to be adaptive, many individuals must be able to use them. It is therefore likely that many such improvements were first discovered culturally, and only later influenced the genetic make-up of the language users by selecting for those individuals who could learn best.

3.5 Self-organization and understanding the origins of language

When the discipline of linguistics was in its infancy, there was much speculation about the origins of language. Many theories existed, but none of these was founded on solid facts. With the increase in our knowledge about language, language change, language development in infants, palaeontology, etc., it has become possible to conduct more comprehensive investigations into the origins and evolution of language. A consensus is forming that anatomically modern *Homo sapiens*, who appeared more than 200,000 years ago, had fully developed language, while *Homo erectus* (from about two million years ago) probably had some form of protolanguage. This allows a period of about two million years for the capacity for language to evolve. In this period numerous anatomical adaptations to the use of language have clearly been made, such as the lowered larynx as well as the subtle and voluntary control over breathing and the movement of the tongue. Often seen as indicative of the evolution of language is increased brain size and complexity (present in the fossil evidence as imprints of brains on the inside of skulls). However, many linguists would argue that most of the innovation has taken place in the use to which the brain is put. There are now areas that seem to be specialized for language, and the human brain is capable, for example, of learning a large vocabulary effortlessly, analysing complex hierarchical structures, and performing complex symbolic thought. Such behavioural changes obviously leave no trace in the fossil record, so the period of time over which they have evolved remains largely speculative, but it must have been fairly short, say, between five hundred thousand and two million years.

This is quite a short period for such complex changes to have occurred. Although some researchers have proposed single mutations that changed a brain incapable of language to a 'language ready brain' (Calvin and Bickerton 2000) and although such saltational change in evolution cannot always be excluded (see, for example, 'A short way to corn' in Gould 1991 for a convincing argument for the saltational origin of maize), I tend to the opinion that the evolution of the human capacity for language has been gradual. But not all properties of language as it occurs today necessarily have to be the result of biological evolution. Other non-biological mechanisms, such as the ones described in the previous section, were also responsible for the emergence of language. The research described here is not the first to investigate these mechanisms. Hurford (1987) and Kirby (1999 and references therein), for example, have already explored the role of population dynamics in explaining certain universals of syntax. They also found that some universals of language might be the result of mechanisms other than biological evolution.

In order to investigate the evolution of language, one therefore has to divide the properties of human language into those that *have* to be explained as the result of biological evolution (an obvious example of this category would be the range of sounds that can be produced by the human vocal tract) and those that can be explained as the result of other processes such as self-organization or cultural evolution. The research described in this book has shown that universal tendencies of vowel systems can be predicted as the result of self-organization, and therefore do not need to be explained as the result of biological evolution. Non-biological mechanisms are likely also to have played an important role in other aspects of language, most notably in syntax.

In thus reducing the number of phenomena that have to be explained as the result of biological evolution (and that have to be genetically determined) one reduces the complexity of the evolution of human language. This makes it more understandable that human language has evolved in the relatively short time that was available.

4.   The Simulation

Simulating the development of a system of speech sounds in a potentially large population of agents requires a computer model that is at the same time realistic and fast. These are two contradictory requirements. Realism can only be increased by the carrying out of extra calculations, which reduces speed. Consequently, it is necessary to make a compromise. The properties that are really essential for getting results that are comparable with human speech will have to be kept, and the rest will have to be sacrificed. However, if realism is sacrificed in a sensible way, the results of the simulation will still be comparable with observations of data from real human languages. Of course, in doing this, one has to keep in mind which parts of the simulation were realistic and which ones were artificial. This chapter describes the computer model that was used for investigating the formation of vowel systems in a population of agents. It also describes and defends the choices that were made between realism and speed. In order that the reader may better understand the reasoning behind these choices, a short history of the simulation is first presented.

4.1 The use of computer simulations

What does it mean to investigate linguistic phenomena with computer simulations? It can be argued that computer simulations can never capture the full complexity of human language, and this would be right. However, one does not need to capture all complexity in order to obtain interesting results. In order to gain an understanding of a phenomenon as complex as natural language, it has to be broken up into more manageable parts.

In fact this process is being carried out in all natural sciences. To investigate a certain phenomenon, one first observes its behaviour. Then one makes a theoretical model of the phenomenon, including which parameters should influence its behaviour, and one makes hypotheses about how the behaviour would change when the parameters are manipulated. Experiments can then be designed to manipulate the different parameters independently, in an artificial, controlled setting. In this way the hypotheses and the theory can be tested and refined iteratively. However, for phenomena as complex as language, it is quite difficult to conduct experiments in the way experiments can be done with simple physical systems. It is difficult to identify which parameters play a role. It is usually not possible to manipulate parameters, even if one suspects that they exist. Also, the interactions between different parameters can be so complex that it does not make sense to manipulate them independently.

One of the big problems of linguistics research is therefore that it is relatively easy to make theories, but that it is very hard to test them. Traditionally, the only way to test linguistic theories was to make linguistic predictions and test with data from natural languages whether the theory held, or whether it was falsified. This is a very complex and time-consuming process and the results of linguistic observations can often be interpreted in different ways. Also, linguistic theories can become so complex that it is not always easy to see what linguistic behaviour they predict.

Computer models are therefore a useful tool for testing the implications of linguistic theories. They do not have difficulties with calculating the consequences of complex theories. Also, parameters in computer models can easily be manipulated. Linguistic theories can be implemented on computers and tested with corpora of real linguistic input. If the behaviour of the computer model corresponds with human behaviour, the underlying theory is not refuted. However, if there is a discrepancy between human behaviour and the behaviour of the model, it is clear that the theory needs revision. In this way, competing theories can be compared. The theory that has the best performance is probably the best model of actual human behaviour.

It is particularly the theories of language as a collective behaviour, such as that of Steels (Steels 1997*b*, Steels 1998*a*) described in the first part of this chapter, and work by, among others, Batali (1998) and Kirby (1998, 1999), that benefit from computer implementations. The results of repeated interactions in a large population of agents are almost impossible to predict without actually modelling them. In recent years, in the field of artificial life (see, for example, Langton 1989, Langton *et al.* 1990), much successful research has been done on similar modelling of biological systems. Results have been achieved that would have been impossible without computer models. The building of computer simulations of linguistic phenomena is therefore justified.

4.2 Purpose of the simulation

The purpose of the simulation is to investigate the emergence of a vowel system in a population of agents that learn to imitate each other as successfully as possible with an open system of vowel sounds. The agents' production, perception, and learning of speech sounds should be as human-like as possible. Each agent should be able to produce, perceive, and remember a set of realistic vowels. It should be able to engage in interactions with other agents and to learn and adapt its system of vowels from these interactions. The number of vowels it knows or their positions should not be determined beforehand. Once an agent has developed a vowel system that works, it should keep this system, without altering it too much. In a group, the agents should be able to generate such a system from scratch. The aim is not to model the exact way in which human vowel systems emerge and change historically, but to investigate whether a population is in principle able to develop a coherent set of vowels from scratch, and whether the sets of vowels that emerge show the same universal tendencies as human vowel systems.

In order to keep the simulation manageable a number of things should *not* be modelled. First of all, the utterances of the agents do not have any meaning. They are just sounds. The goal of the agents is to imitate the other agents as well as possible. This is considered to be basic to language; only if you are capable of identifying and imitating the other speaker's sounds can you begin to learn the meaning that is attached to the sounds. Other researchers (see, for example, Steels 1997*a*, Steels and Vogt 1997, Gasser 1998) are investigating the origins of meaning and the way in which meanings can be coupled to words.

The question why agents would want to communicate with language, and thus to imitate, is not posed either. In the work presented here, the need for communication with language is assumed as a given. Other researchers (for example, Werner and Dyer 1991, Hauser 1997, de Jong 1998) are investigating the origins of communication with language. Having the agents develop the need to imitate would complicate the model needlessly; this need is therefore pre-programmed.

The drive to add new sounds to the inventory is also pre-programmed. It is needed, because the agents start out with empty sound systems, but still have an urge to imitate. It is therefore necessary to add new sounds every once in a while, in order to get the imitations started. In a natural language one can imagine that addition of new sounds is either a by-product of the disappearance of phonetic context or is driven by the need to distinguish as many meanings as possible, while keeping the length of utterances low. But when it is necessary to make more distinctions, effective use of the available acoustic space is necessary. This is an example of a case where one part of language, the lexicon, exerts pressure on another part of language, the sound system.

The many subtle social factors that determine the use and change of human speech sounds are also not modelled, for two reasons. First, they are extremely hard to model. There is no clear picture of which factors are important, nor of how, exactly, they influence the use of sounds in human languages. Secondly, social factors are important for explaining the specific historical sound changes that particular human languages have undergone, but for the sake of modelling it is assumed that these factors can be considered random fluctuations. As far as is known, social factors can determine which one of a number of variations will be chosen. However, the variation itself will be random (but biased by factors such as articulatory ease and perceptual distinctiveness).

Finally, only utterances of single vowels are modelled. This has the advantage of being easily implementable, but the disadvantage of being unrealistic. However, vowel systems are often investigated without taking into account the contexts in which the vowels can appear. This is true for much of the work on explaining the universals of vowel systems (Liljencrants and Lindblom 1972, Schwartz, Boë, Vallée, and Abry 1997). The predictions of these models are quite accurate, so it can safely be concluded that for predicting vowel systems the context in which the vowels can appear does not play a very important role. However, the context *does* influence the possible ways in which vowels can change historically. In order to model realistic historical sound change, sequences of sounds will have to be modelled. This means that although the model presented here can in principle be used to predict vowel systems, it cannot be used to model *change* of vowel systems accurately.

4.2.1 *Agent architecture*

The agents should be equipped with an accurate articulatory vowel synthesizer, a realistic model of perception, and a memory to store a list of vowels (see Figure 4.1). In the system used here, vowels are stored in terms of a prototypical acoustic signal and a prototypical articulatory position per vowel phoneme. The articulatory prototype of a vowel consists of the values for the three major vowel parameters, position, height, and rounding. The acoustic signal consists of the first four formant frequencies of the vowel. The reason for storing articulatory representations of vowels and for using an articulatory synthesizer to produce acoustic signals, rather than just storing acoustic representations of vowels (as Berrah (1998) does), is that this is probably the most realistic way. People have control over the way they move their articulators, not over the sounds they perceive. It would therefore seem likely that children have to learn which sounds are produced for which articulatory movements. As the mapping between acoustic signals and articulatory gestures is complex, this is a non-trivial learning task. Also, when an unknown sound is heard, it is unlikely that it can be reproduced exactly, because it has to be analysed first in terms of articulator movements. Finally, if one uses an articulatory synthesizer, one does not have to worry about the limits of the acoustic space available for communication. The limits of the acoustic space are automatically determined by the limits of the articulators.

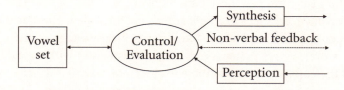

Figure 4.1. Agent architecture

The acoustic signal associated with the articulatory prototype is used for recognition only. Incoming signals are compared with the stored acoustic signals, instead of with signals that are generated from the articulatory prototypes with the articulatory synthesizer. This is done to reduce the amount of computation needed. Every time the agent produces a vowel, however, a new acoustic signal is generated with the articulatory synthesizer, with noise added.

Depending on the outcome of the interactions with other agents, the agent can either add or remove prototypes from its memory, or shift existing prototypes. The exact mechanisms for producing and perceiving vowels, as well as the exact interactions between the agents, are described in the sections that follow.

Imitation was chosen as a model for investigating the emergence of sound systems in a population because it is the simplest way to capture the complexity of learning a sound system. It does involve recognizing and distinguishing sounds, but there does not have to be meaning to the sounds. There is also no need for explicit optimization of the vowel system. However, as (near-)optimal vowel systems are easier to learn and imitate than non-optimal sound systems, they have the advantage and will be adopted by the agents more easily. The human-like perception and production of speech will ensure that systems that are optimal for the agents are also optimal for humans. Self-organization thus ensures that near-optimal systems are found more frequently than sub-optimal ones. Optimal systems could be considered *attractors* of the dynamic system that is formed by the agents (their perception and their production) and the interactions between the agents.

4.3 The articulatory model

The articulatory model of the agents maps the articulatory representation of vowels to an acoustic representation. The articulatory representation consists of three parameters, *position*, *height*, and *rounding*, corresponding to the three major vowel parameters (Ladefoged and Maddieson 1996, ch. 9). They are real numbers between zero and one. As regards position, corresponding to the position of the tongue in the front–back dimension, zero means furthest to the front, while one means furthest to the back. As regards height, corresponding to the height of the highest point of the tongue, and thus the openness of the vowel, zero means most open, while one means most closed. Rounding corresponds to the rounding of the lips. Zero means most spread, while one means most rounded. Thus the vowel [a] has values $(0, 0, 0)$ for its parameters (position, height, rounding) while [i] has $(0, 1, 0)$ and [u] has $(1, 1, 1)$.

The acoustic signals that are exchanged between agents are represented by the first four formant frequencies (F_1, F_2, F_3, F_4). Formants are the peaks in a vowel's frequency spectrum. The first three or four are usually considered to be sufficient to represent a vowel. As calculating formants can be done much more quickly than calculating an actual signal, this increases the speed of the simulation. Also, the measure of perceptual distance that was used (see the next section) was based on formant frequencies. Obviously, a real vowel signal contains much more information than just the formant frequencies. Other properties of the vowel signal are, for example, volume and frequency contours, duration, voicing characteristics, and formant bandwidths. Although some of these properties do have linguistic relevance, they do not influence the perception of the vowel *quality* much. Vowel quality is the only property investigated in this book.

The articulatory model has to be realistic as well as fast. It has to be realistic so that the results of the simulations can be compared with observations of real languages and it has to be fast so that the simulations can be run interactively. A full articulatory synthesizer, such as that used by Maeda (1989) or Mermelstein (1973), was therefore out of the question. Modelling the area function of the vocal tract from the large number of degrees of freedom of these models and then calculating the formant frequencies for the area function would be too computationally intensive. Furthermore, it was not clear how to map the rather abstract parameters of position, height, and rounding to the degrees of freedom of these models.

It was therefore decided to calculate the formant frequencies from the articulator positions directly. This can be done with an interpolation func-

$$
\begin{aligned}
F_1 = &\ ((-392+392r)h^2 + (596-668r)h + (-146+166r))p^2 \\
&+ ((348-348r)h^2 + (-494+606r)h + (141-175r))p \\
&+ ((340-72r)h^2 + (-796+108r)h + (708-38r)) \\
F_2 = &\ ((-1200+1208r)h^2 + (1320-1328r)h + (118-158r))p^2 \\
&+ ((1864-1488r)h^2 + (-2644+1510r)h + (-561+221r)p \\
&+ ((-670+490r)h^2 + (1355-697r)h + (1517-117r)) \\
F_3 = &\ ((604-604r)h^2 + (1038-1178r)h + (246+566r))p^2 \\
&+ ((-1150+1262r)h^2 + (-1443+1313r)h + (-317-483r))p \\
&+ ((1130-836r)h^2 + (-315+44r)h + (2427-127r)) \\
F_4 = &\ ((-1120+16r)h^2 + (1696-180r)h + (500+522r))p^2 \\
&+ ((-140+240r)h^2 + (-578+214r)h + (-692-419r))p \\
&+ ((1480-602r)h^2 + (-1220+289r)h + (3678-178r))
\end{aligned}
$$

FIGURE 4.2. Synthesizer equations

tion. The interpolation was based on information on formant frequencies of a large number of vowels in Vallée's thesis (Vallée 1994, pp. 162–164). These vowels had been artificially generated using the Maeda articulatory synthesizer. A subset of these vowels, for three degrees of position and height and for two degrees of rounding, was used. The values of the articulatory parameters were assigned to the vowels according to the phonetic symbols that were used in Vallée's list.

As there were three degrees of position and height, a quadratic interpolation had to be used for these dimensions. There were only two degrees of rounding in the data set, so here a linear interpolation was used. The resulting three-dimensional, quadratic-linear interpolation function is given in Figure 4.2.

Although this is a rather crude way of solving the problem of articulatory synthesis, it is nevertheless an effective one. The formant patterns that can be generated sound natural to human ears if synthesized. Even vowels that were not used as data points, such as [ɛ] or [ɔ], sound natural. All formant frequencies that can be generated lie within the formant space that can be generated by humans (Figure 4.3). The main advantage of the method, however, is that it is fast. Only 70 multiplications and 68 additions are required to calculate the four formant frequencies of one vowel: 17 multiplications and additions per formant and two more multiplications

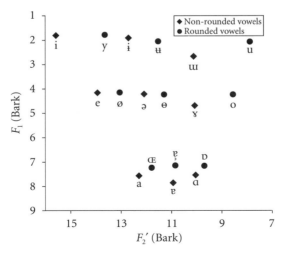

FIGURE 4.3. Vowels in F_1–F_2' space

for calculating p^2 and h^2. This makes the articulatory model very well suited for the kinds of simulations that have to be done, in which very many interactions between agents have to be modelled in a limited time.

4.3.1 *The addition of noise*

In order to make the simulation more realistic the synthesis of the signal will have to be made noisy. In human communication, no signal will ever be exactly the same as a previously generated signal, owing to slight perturbations in articulation, differences between speakers, and environmental noise. Two sources of noise were therefore added to the synthesizer: articulatory noise and acoustic noise. Articulatory noise was modelled by adding a small random value to all three articulatory parameters. This value is taken from the uniform distribution with the range:

$$\left[-\frac{\psi_{art}}{2}, \frac{\psi_{art}}{2} \right),$$

where ψ_{art} is the amount of articulatory noise present, a parameter of the simulation. Acoustic noise is added by shifting formant frequencies up or down by a random amount. As human perception of pitch is logarithmic, this means that in order to have the same auditory effect, higher frequencies will have to be shifted more than lower frequencies. This is done in the following way. For every formant i, a random value v_i is taken from the uniform distribution:

$$\left[-\frac{\psi_{ac}}{2}, \frac{\psi_{ac}}{2} \right),$$

where ψ_{ac} is the amount of acoustic noise present, also a parameter of the simulation. Now every formant is modified in the following way:

$$F_i = F_i(1+v_i), \tag{4.1}$$

where F_i is the originally calculated formant frequency (expressed in hertz) and F_i is the formant frequency with noise. This causes the formants to be shifted proportionally to their frequency.

With this articulatory model, agents are able to produce vowels in a continuous acoustic and articulatory space. The mapping between articulatory parameters and acoustic parameters is both fast and realistic. The addition of noise to either articulatory or acoustic parameters ensures that no two signals will ever be produced that are exactly the same. Although the random noise is uniformly distributed, it is nevertheless probably a good model of variation of human speech. This makes the articulatory synthesizer very well suited for the research goals being pursued.

4.4 The perception model

Agents should not only be able to produce vowels in a realistic way but also perceive vowels in a human-like way. Humans tend to analyse speech sounds they hear in terms of sounds they already know. Speech sounds that are unlike, but close to, sounds they already know will be interpreted as familiar speech sounds. A speaker of English, for example, will confuse the French vowel /y/ with either /i/ or /u/. In French these three sounds contrast: /ny/ 'nu' (naked), /ni/ 'nid' (nest), and /nu/ 'nous' (we) are different words, but in English the /y/ does not appear, whereas /i/ and /u/ do. Whenever (linguistically naïve) English speakers hear /y/, for example in the French word 'nu', they will think they heard either /i/ (as in 'knee') or /u/ (as in 'gnu') depending on the context.

Research into the perception of consonants (Cooper *et al.* 1976, Liberman *et al.* 1976) has shown that when acoustic signals, consisting of artificially generated consonant–vowel sequences, are changed continuously, subjects will perceive one consonant for one range of parameter settings, and other consonants for other settings of the parameter. The perception changes abruptly when the parameter changes from one range to the other. Which consonants are perceived for given parameter settings depends on the native language of the subjects. Apparently humans perceive speech in terms of *prototypical* sounds. In other parts of language, such as syntax and semantics, prototypical perception seems to take place as well (see, for example, Comrie 1981, Lakoff 1987).

The agents should display similar behaviour. They have a list of vowel prototypes. Whenever they perceive an acoustic signal, they find the (acoustic) prototype that is closest to the signal they perceived. This prototype is then considered the phoneme that was heard, even though in fact it can sound quite different, especially if the agent has very few prototypes. The crucial part of recognizing acoustic signals is therefore calculating their distance to the acoustic prototypes. Whenever the distance function is realistic, the perception will be realistic.

4.4.1 *Calculating the distance between vowels*

The distance function is based on a weighted Euclidean distance between representations of vowels consisting of the first formant frequency and the effective second formant frequency, measured in Barks.[1] The notion of the *effective second formant* is inspired by the way human perception of vowels works. If human subjects are asked to approximate vowel sounds as closely as possible, using only two formant frequencies, it is found that the first formant frequency chosen corresponds closely with the first formant frequency of the vowel. However, the second formant frequency chosen does not always correspond to the position of the second formant frequency in the actual signal. Sometimes it is located between the second and the third formant frequencies, sometimes even between the third and the fourth (Carlson *et al.* 1970). The perception of a four-formant pattern as a pattern of two formants is caused by the fact that in the high-frequency range, human hearing is not able to resolve peaks with narrow bandwidth. The signals at different frequencies effectively merge into each other. If there are two or more peaks close together in the signal, they will actually be observed as one wide peak, located approximately midway between the two peaks. It should be noted, however, that not all patterns of four formants are perceived as two-formant patterns. If the higher formant peaks are sufficiently far apart, they will be perceived separately. The effective second formant model is therefore not a totally accurate model of human perception. However, it does work most of the time.

There are different ways of calculating the effective second formant frequency. The one that was used here is a slightly adapted version of the one used at the Institut de Communication Parlée of Grenoble (Mantakas *et al.* 1986, Boë *et al.* 1995). This particular model was adopted because it gives natural results and because it facilitates comparison of the results of the simulations presented here with the Grenoble simulations (Vallée 1994, Boë *et al.* 1995, Schwartz, Boë, Vallée, and Abry 1997, Berrah 1998).

The effective second formant, F_2', is calculated as a non-linear, weighted sum of the second, third, and fourth formants. It is based on a critical distance between formant peaks. This critical distance models bandwidth of the human perception at the higher frequencies (and therefore the

---

[1] The Bark scale is an (approximately) logarithmic frequency scale that models the human perception of pitch. Pairs of sounds that are perceived to have equal distance in pitch have equal distance in Barks, no matter what their absolute frequency is.

confusion of formant peaks). Just as in the other work using this calculation, the critical distance is taken to be 3.5 Barks. If the distance between
F_2 and F_3 is more than the critical distance, the actual F_2 is used as F_2'. If
the distance between F_2 and F_3 is smaller than the critical distance, but the
distance between F_2 and F_4 is more than the critical distance, then F_2' is
taken to be a weighted average of F_2 and F_3. If the distance between F_2 and
F_4 is also less than the critical distance, then F_2' is taken to be the weighted
average of either F_2 and F_3 or F_3 and F_4, whichever are closer together.

The weights in the original formula were determined by the strengths
of the formant peaks. As the articulatory model of the agents does not
calculate the strengths of the formants, the weights are calculated depending on the distance between the formants (as, in general, formants that are
close to other formants tend to be stronger). This is done as follows:

$$w_1 = \frac{c - (F_3 - F_2)}{c} \tag{4.2}$$

$$w_2 = \frac{(F_4 - F_3) - (F_3 - F_2)}{F_4 - F_2}, \tag{4.3}$$

where c is the critical distance. The calculation of F_2' can then be expressed
in the following formula:

$$F_2' = \begin{cases} F_2, & \text{if } F_3 - F_2 > c \\ \dfrac{(2 - w_1)F_2 + w_1 F_3}{2}, & \text{if } F_3 - F_2 \le c \text{ and } F_4 - F_2 > c \\ \dfrac{w_2 F_2 + (2 - w_2)F_3}{2} - 1, & \text{if } F_4 - F_2 \le c \text{ and } F_3 - F_2 < F_4 - F_3 \\ \dfrac{(2 + w_2)F_3 - w_2 F_4}{2} - 1, & \text{if } F_4 - F_2 \le c \text{ and } F_3 - F_2 \ge F_4 - F_3, \end{cases} \tag{4.4}$$

and the distance between two vowels can be calculated as follows:

$$D = \sqrt{(F_1^a - F_1^b)^2 + \lambda (F_2^{a'} - F_2^{b'})^2}. \tag{4.5}$$

In this formula, the parameter λ represents the factor with which the
effective second formant is weighted relative to the first formant. As F_1 is
proportional to vowel height, and F_2' proportional to vowel position, this

factor tends to determine the accuracy with which agents can distinguish between different vowel positions and different vowel heights. The higher λ is, the more distinctions an agent will be able to make in the front–back dimension as opposed to the high–low dimension. Experiments with determining maximally dispersed vowel systems (Vallée 1994, Schwartz, Boë, Vallée, and Abry 1997) as well as independent data from human production of vowels (Lindblom and Lubker 1985) seem to indicate that this factor should be approximately 0.3.

The way in which the weights w_1 and w_2 are calculated and used in this work was found to introduce some irregularities in the perceptual space. Because for different configurations of the four–formant frequencies, different functions are used for calculating the effective second formant, discontinuities sometimes arise in F_2' when the formant pattern itself changes continuously. It was found that the influence on the qualitative outcome of the experiments was not important, and it appears that this irregularity corresponds with a perceptual effect. The irregularity was slightly compensated for by subtracting one from the effective second formant value in the last two cases in equation 4.4. Whenever it has influenced the results of the simulations this will be noted. However, for future research it is advisable to use a weighting function that does not have discontinuities in order to avoid all problems.

The distance function is used to calculate the distances between the perceived signal and the acoustic prototypes of all the vowels. The agent recognizes the vowel that is closest to the perceived signal. As the distance function assigns large distances to signals that are perceived very differently by humans and small distances to signals that are perceived to be very similar by humans, it is a good model of human perception. The distance function is also used in approximating a new, unknown signal. The distance between the unknown signal and a newly added vowel is minimized using an algorithm that is described in more detail in the next section.

4.5 The imitation game

The articulatory model and the perception model determine the kinds of sounds the agents can produce and how they perceive them. The dynamics of the model, however, are determined by the way the agents use these sounds. In the simulations presented here, sounds are used in so-called *imitation games*. Imitation games are played between two agents whose goal is to imitate the other agent as well as possible. The imitation game is based on the idea of language games as introduced by Steels (1995, 1997*b*, 1998*a*). Language games are interactions between two (or more) agents that follow definite rules and of which it can be determined unequivocally whether they were successful or not. Depending on the outcome of the language games, the agents update their knowledge of the language. Steels was inspired by Wittgenstein's philosophical theories (Wittgenstein 1967) as well as by research by Suzuki and Kaneko (1994) on artificial bird songs when developing the idea of language games. The 'rules' of the imitation game, as well as the agents' reaction to them, are described in this section and illustrated in Figure 4.4.

For an imitation game, two agents are randomly chosen from the population. One of these will be given the role of *initiator*, the other the role of *imitator*. The initiator randomly chooses a vowel from its inventory. It then synthesizes the acoustic signal that corresponds to this vowel while noise is added to it. The imitator, who hears the perturbed signal, analyses it in terms of the vowels in its inventory. It finds the closest one (using the distance measure described in the previous section) and then synthesizes the acoustic signal that corresponds to this vowel, also adding noise. Note that even without the presence of noise, the imitation can sound quite different from the sound produced by the initiator, especially when the vowel inventories of the two agents are small and different. The initiator in

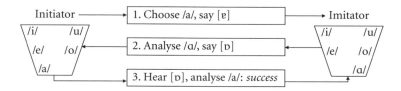

FIGURE 4.4. Example of the imitation game

Note: The process is as follows. First the initiator chooses a random vowel (in this case /a/) from its repertoire, produces it with its synthesizer, adding noise (it becomes [ɐ]). Secondly, the imitator analyses this sound in terms of *its* vowels and synthesizes the recognized vowel (/ɑ/) also adding noise (it becomes [ɒ]). Then the initiator listens to the imitator's sound, analyses it, and checks if the recognized vowel is the same as the original one (here, [ɒ] is analysed as /a/, so the game is successful). If the [ɒ] had been perceived closer to /o/, then the game would have been a failure. The vowel systems shown are representative examples. In reality, agents' vowel systems can contain all possible vowels and may contain different numbers of vowels.

turn listens to this signal and analyses it in the same way. If it turns out that the closest match to the signal it heard is the same vowel prototype as the one it originally used to initiate the game, the imitation game is successful. If the vowel the initiator perceives is a different one from the one it produced, there is confusion and the imitation game is a failure. The initiator then communicates the success or the failure to the imitator using non-linguistic communication. This might seem unrealistic, as humans do not learn language by being told that their utterances are right or wrong all the time. However, the non-verbal feedback is only an abstract way of letting the imitator know whether its imitation was right. In actual human communication, this feedback could be derived from whether the intended goal of the communication has been achieved. If someone does not use the right sounds in an utterance, he or she will not be understood and it will be clear that the communication was a failure. The appropriate reaction would then be to update his or her knowledge of the sounds.

The goal of the agents is to imitate each other as well as possible with a repertoire of sounds that is as large as possible. For this they need to develop repertoires of sounds that are similar to the ones of the other agents. The only way they can learn about the other agents' repertoires is through the imitation games. They should therefore use the outcome of the imitation games for improving their vowel systems. First of all, both the imitator and the initiator keep track of the number of times each of their vowels has been used and the number of times it has been used in successful imitation games. These are called the *use* and *success* counts, respectively. The ratio of these two counts is a measure of the successfulness of a vowel. The successfulness of a vowel is mainly determined by how well it is shared by all agents in the population. If not many agents share it, it will not be imitated successfully very often. On the other hand, if many agents do share it, it will be imitated successfully most of the time.

The imitator makes the most important changes to its vowel system in response to the imitation game. If the imitation game was successful, it shifts the vowel that was used so that its acoustic signal will match the observed acoustic signal more closely. This is done in order to improve coherence in the population. Changing pronunciation in order to match others more closely is also necessary for children learning a language. As the agents can only directly manipulate the articulatory representations of vowels, and not their acoustic ones, they have to use a trick in order to optimize the acoustic signal of the vowel. The trick is similar to the way people learning a new language try out small variations on an unfamiliar sound in order to improve its pronunciation. It consists of trying out the six neighbours of the vowel in articulatory space and keeping the one that most closely matches the acoustic signal. The six neighbours of a vowel are the vowels that differ from it in each of its three articulatory parameters by a specific small amount in either the negative or positive direction. The value of the small amount with which vowels are shifted is a parameter of the simulation that can be controlled by the experimenter (but which in the experiments presented in this book is kept at 0.03).

If the imitation game was unsuccessful, there are two possible actions the imitator can undertake. If the vowel it used has been successful in the past (that is, it has a high success/use ratio) this means that there must be other agents that are using it. Changing it too much might therefore not be a very good idea. The best assumption to make about why the imitation game failed is that the other agent has two vowels in the same space where this agent only has one. The course of action to take is hence to add a new vowel to the inventory that closely matches the acoustic signal that was observed. It is not possible to find the right articulatory parameters from an acoustic signal directly. A new vowel is therefore added in the middle of the articulatory space (all articulatory parameters are set to 0.5) and the vowel is shifted closer to the acoustic signal repeatedly in the same way as described in the previous paragraph. This is repeated until no more improvement is possible, the processes described being illustrated in Figure 4.5.

The other possible case is where the vowel was unsuccessful in previous imitation games. Then it is assumed that it is not shared by other agents,

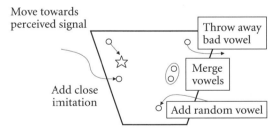

FIGURE 4.5. Changes an agent can make to its vowel system

Note: Circles indicate vowels in the agent's repertoire (both articulatory and acoustic aspect) while the star indicates the position (in acoustic space) of the signal the agent has just perceived.

and it is shifted towards the acoustic signal that was observed, in the hope of bringing it close enough so that next time it will be successful. The threshold above which vowels are considered successful enough, so that a new phoneme will have to be added, is another parameter of the simulation, with a standard value of 0.5.

The agents can also make modifications to their vowel inventories that are not directly driven by the outcome of a particular imitation game. The first modification is a 'clean-up' of the vowel system. In this clean-up all vowels that have been used a minimum number of times, so they have had the occasion to be tested, and the successfulness of which is still lower than a threshold, are removed from the inventory. Both the threshold and the minimum number of times a phoneme has to be used are parameters of the simulation (with values set to 0.7 and 5, respectively). An agent is cleaned up with a probability of 0.1 every imitation game. Another modification is that two vowels in the inventory will be merged if they come so close in either articulatory or acoustic space that they will always be confused by the noise that is added to the articulations (the minimal articulatory distance is 0.17 and the minimal acoustic distance is two times the maximum distance over which the signal can be shifted owing to noise). This was found to be necessary to prevent large numbers of unsuccessful vowels clustering around the positions where only one good vowel was necessary. Merging is done by throwing away the worse one of the two vowels that are too close. The use and success counts of the vowel that is kept are increased by the use and success counts of the vowel that was thrown away. The last modification that agents can make to their inventories is to add a new random vowel. This is done with a low probability (1 per cent) that is also a parameter of the simulation. It is done in order to keep a pressure on the agent to utilize the acoustic space maximally.

All of these actions use only local information. Agents only use information about the signals they perceive and the information they have about their own vowel systems. The modifications to the vowel system do not use information about the vowel system as a whole, only about individual vowels or about neighbouring vowels that are close together (in the case of merging). The modifications the agents can make do not require an unrealistic amount of computation, either. So, even though the simulation described in this book is not and does not pretend to be an accurate model of human language learning, no completely unrealistic hat-tricks were used to make the sound system emerge either.

5. Results

Running the simulation described in the previous chapter with the right parameter settings did result in natural vowel systems. Shared sets of vowels were obtained, so that imitation was highly successful. The vowel systems that emerged from the simulations were similar to those most frequently found in the languages of the world. However, it is hard to define similarity in the context of these simulations. It is easy to obtain an impressionistic idea of how realistic the agents' inventories are by making a scatter plot of the agents' vowels, using the first and effective second formant as coordinates. This is the way the outcomes of the simulations are usually plotted in this book. But the number of vowel clusters that emerge is not fixed, even for given parameter values, and not all agents in the population have exactly the same vowel system. It is therefore very hard to conduct a rigorous statistical analysis of the outcomes of the simulations.

This chapter first presents an impression of the behaviour of the simulations. This is followed by two comparisons of the quality and realism of systems that result from different runs of the simulation. First, emerged vowel systems are compared with random ones and explicitly optimized ones, by using different measures of the system. Secondly, the classification of the emerged systems is compared with classifications of human vowel systems.

5.1 A first example

The aim of the simulations is to see whether a population of agents is able to generate a shared system of speech sounds and whether these systems will resemble human sound systems. Therefore, when the simulation is started, the agents' vowel inventories are empty. In the course of the imitation games, they will fill their inventories and update them according to the result of the imitation games they play with the other agents. An example of the emergence of a vowel system in a population of 20 agents is shown in Figure 5.1.

The frames in Figure 5.1 have been made by plotting all vowels of all agents in a two-dimensional acoustic space. The frequency of the first form-ant determines the y-coordinate of each point and the frequency of the effective second formant determines the x-coordinate. Both frequencies are expressed in Barks. The values increase from top to bottom and from right to left, respectively, so that the positions of the points in the graph correspond to the positions the corresponding vowels are traditionally given in phonetic literature. Clusters mean that most of the agents of the population have a vowel in this region of the acoustic space. The space

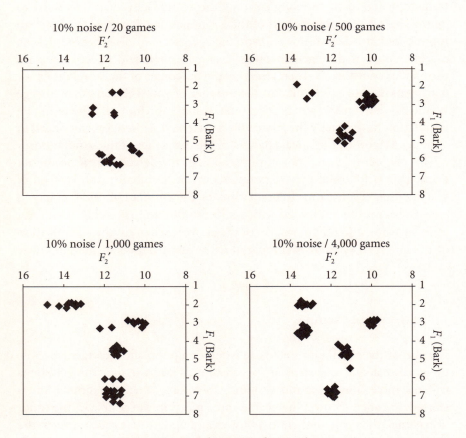

FIGURE 5.1. Development of a vowel system

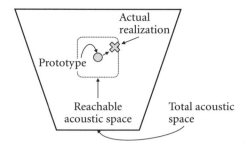

FIGURE 5.2. What happens to a vowel if noise is added to it

between clusters indicates that these vowels are distinct from the other vowels in all agents' repertoires. Apparently, however, the agents do not have exactly the same realization of a vowel. This is also the case with human speakers, all of whom pronounce a given vowel slightly differently as well, even when it is the same individual producing vowels in isolation (see Figure 5.3). One also has to keep in mind that the points in the graphs are the acoustic representations of the vowel prototypes to which no noise is added. Whenever agents play an imitation game, noise is added to their

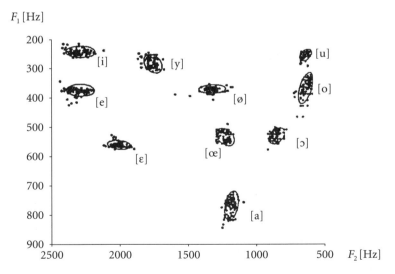

FIGURE 5.3. Vowel system of French, produced as isolated vowels by a single male speaker
Source: Adapted, with permission, from Robert-Ribes (1995) via Glotin (1995).
Note: Cf. Figure 5.19.

utterances, so that the actual realizations of the vowels might be shifted somewhat from the point represented in the graph (see Figure 5.2).

The first frame in Figure 5.1 shows the system after 20 imitation games with 10 per cent acoustic noise. The most important process so far has been the random addition of vowels. The agents that initiated the imitation game mostly had empty vowel inventories, and therefore had to invent random vowels. For the imitator there are two possibilities. It either had an empty repertoire and had to create a new vowel that is a good imitation of the vowel it heard, or it had only one vowel in its repertoire which was necessarily used. The first case causes pairs of close points in the graph. The second case will lead to a successful imitation game, because both agents have only one vowel in their repertoire, even though the sounds that are used might sound quite different to human ears. The successfulness of the imitation game will cause the imitator's vowel to be shifted slightly towards the initiator's one. Thus vowels are expected to cluster.

Because only few imitation games have been played, the sounds have not clustered in the first frame, but in the second frame one can observe emerging clusters. This happens after some 500 imitation games. At this point the most important process is the moving closer together of the different agents' vowel prototypes. Usually, imitation games will be successful, and the result will be that vowel prototypes are shifted closer together. More clusters have formed in the meantime, owing to the random addition of vowels that continues to take place with low probability. Therefore, some agents will have more vowels than others and sometimes imitation games will fail, forcing other agents to add vowels as well.

The third frame shows the vowel system after 1,000 imitation games. The most important process in this phase is the random addition of new vowels. Every once in a while, a random vowel is added to one of the agents and if it is sufficiently different from already existing vowels, the other agents quickly create corresponding vowels in their vowel inventories. If it is not sufficiently different from the other vowels, its success/use ratio will drop quickly and it will be removed from the agent's inventory. New vowels can thus only be successful if there is sufficient room in the acoustic space. After a certain number of vowels have been added, there is no more space, and the vowel inventories of the agents do not change any further.

This is the situation in frame 4, after 4,000 imitation games. Here one observes a natural-looking vowel system, where there are a number of compact clusters with sufficient space in between. All agents have a vowel in all the clusters, meaning that imitation will almost always be successful. The most important process in this phase is shifting of vowels. As vowels are always generated with some noise, no two agents will produce exactly the same signal, ever. Therefore agents will always shift their vowels a little bit in response to an imitation game. This implies that the resulting vowel system is not completely static. Clusters can still shift, and if they shift in such a way that new space is opened, a new vowel might be added. If they shift in such a way that two clusters come close together, they might merge. However, clusters will not disperse over time, as would be expected if movement was totally random. Vowel prototypes are always attracted to each other, so they cannot move too far from one another.

The size of the clusters is determined by the noise that is added to the acoustic signal. In the simulation described above, the acoustic noise parameter was 10 per cent. This corresponds to a maximal shift of 0.6 Bark in the graph. The population size was 20 agents. These parameters will be the same for most of the other experiments presented in this book, except where indicated.

In order to obtain an idea of what different systems can be obtained with the simulation, another vowel system is given in Figure 5.4. The only difference between this run of the simulation and the previous one is that the acoustic noise was set to 20 per cent instead of 10 per cent. Owing to

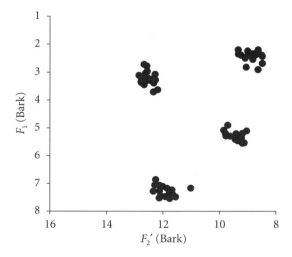

FIGURE 5.4. System obtained with 20 per cent noise

the higher noise level the acoustic realizations of vowels are spread out over a larger part of the acoustic space, so that vowels are confused more easily. This means that there will be fewer clusters, and the clusters are farther apart. Because of the less perfect realization of vowels, the imitations of the agents will be less perfect as well and the clusters will be bigger. Both phenomena can be observed in Figure 5.4.

5.2 Analysis of simulation results

What do these results mean? The vowel systems that form do look like vowel systems that one finds in human languages. Figure 5.3 shows measurements of the vowels of French produced by a single male speaker. They are plotted in the same way as those in the simulations, except that the axes are linear and not logarithmic, which causes the picture to become stretched in the horizontal dimension towards the [i], and in the vertical dimension towards the [a]. The similarities between the simulation results and the real system are striking. This indicates that the model is sufficiently realistic with respect to the distribution of realizations of vowels in acoustic space. However, a somewhat less impressionistic measure is needed in order to make an objective evaluation of the results of the simulations. As has been said above, this comparison has been done in two ways: by comparing the classification of emerged systems with the classification of real human systems and with optimal and random systems. The comparison with artificially generated optimal and random systems is presented first. The comparison with human vowel systems is presented in section 5.6.

5.2.1 *Energy of a vowel system*

The vowel systems can be compared using different objective measures. The first of these is Liljencrants and Lindblom's (1972) energy function (already presented in Chapter 2, equation 2.1, but repeated here for reference).

$$E = \sum_{i=1}^{n-1} \sum_{j=0}^{i-1} \frac{1}{r_{ij}^2} \tag{5.1}$$

where E is the energy of the system, n is the number of vowels in the system, and r_{ij} is the distance (according to the measure of distance presented in

Chapter 4) between vowels *i* and *j*. This function gives a high value if vowels are close together, and a low value if vowels are far apart. Its minimum value is reached when the vowels are maximally dispersed. Liljencrants and Lindblom (1972) found that minimizing this energy function results in a realistic (and frequently occurring) vowel system. Of course, in reality one will rarely find human vowel systems that are completely optimally dispersed and that consequently have minimal energy. However, their energy will tend to be low. It will therefore be assumed that low energy means a realistic vowel system. It must be noted, however, that only the energies of systems with equal numbers of vowels can be compared. The energy function sums over a number of distances that increases with the square of the number of vowels in the systems. The more vowels there are in a system, the higher the energy of the system will be, even if the distances between all the vowels are equal. This was not a problem in Liljencrants and Lindblom's (1972) simulation, nor in subsequent work that optimizes vowel systems with a similar energy function (Vallée 1994, Schwartz, Boë, Vallée, and Abry 1997). It should also not be a problem here, but one should exercise caution when using the energy function to compare runs of the simulation, because they usually contain agents with different numbers of vowels.

5.2.2 *Success of imitation*

The second measure is the success of imitation the agents can achieve. This is calculated by checking for every vowel of every agent in the population whether it will be imitated correctly by the other agents in the population. The number of correct imitations relative to the number of possible pairs of agents then gives a measure of the coherence of the agents' sound systems.

One could imagine a hypothetical vowel system that has either low energy and low imitation success, or high energy and high imitation success. These systems will not be realistic. The first will have dispersed vowels, but clusters which are about as big as the distance between the clusters, and the second will have small clusters, but these clusters will reside in only a small part of the acoustic space. Both systems would be very sensitive to noise. However, if a system has both a high imitation success and a low energy, it is a realistic vowel system, as its vowel clusters will be dispersed (for low energy) and compact (for high imitative success).

5.2.3 *Analysis of emerged systems*

First the systems that are generated by the simulation will be investigated. For this the same parameter settings as for the simulations in the previous section will be used. Systems with acoustic noise of 10 per cent and 20 per cent will be investigated. As it was found that systems in simulations with higher amounts of acoustic noise developed more slowly, a higher value for the insertion of new phonemes of 0.1 was used for the case of 20 per cent noise. The results for the simulation with 10 per cent noise are presented in Figure 5.5. This figure presents the distribution of the success, the number of vowels, and the average energy over 1,000 runs of the simulation. The success was calculated as the running average over the imitation games and was calculated as follows:

$$s_{av} \leftarrow 0.99s_{av} + 0.01s_t, \tag{5.2}$$

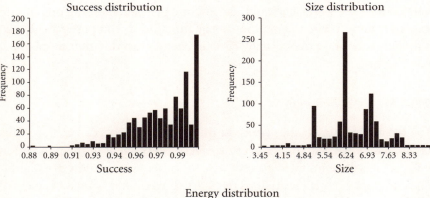

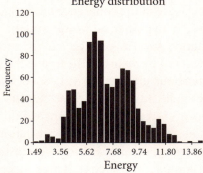

FIGURE 5.5. Success, size, and energy of a 10 per cent noise system

where s_{av} is the running average of the success and s_t is 1 if the imitation game that was just played was successful and 0 if it was a failure. This gives a good estimate of the success of imitation (same average and standard deviation) and requires fewer calculations than exhaustively calculating the successes of all possible interactions between all agents. The number of vowels is the average number of vowels in the agents in a population. The average energy is the average over the energies of the vowel systems of all the agents in the population. The population size was 20 agents.

Although the average of success in Figure 5.5 is 0.973 with standard deviation 0.023, it can be seen that complete success occurs most often. The average of the average vowel system size of the populations is 6.21, with standard deviation 0.82, but it is not distributed normally. The distribution has peaks at integer sizes five, six, and seven. Apparently the simulation has a tendency to converge towards systems where all agents have an equal number of vowels—five, six, or seven in this case. The average energy has an average of 6.75, with a standard deviation of 2.11. The energy also does not follow the normal distribution. One can observe several peaks. These probably indicate different possible configurations for systems consisting of five, six, and seven vowels. The different possible 'minimal' configurations for systems consisting of six vowels are investigated in more detail in the section on optimal systems below and in section 5.6 in the comparison with real human vowel systems.

The case of 20 per cent noise is illustrated in Figure 5.6. The average success is 0.982, with a standard deviation of 0.027. As can be seen in the figure, complete success occurs most frequently. The average size of the agents' vowel inventories seems to cluster around three peaks, for populations sharing two, three, and four vowels respectively. Half of the simulations end up with two-vowel systems and half with three- or four-vowel systems. Again integer numbers are preferred, in this case reflecting the fact that all agents in the population have the same number of vowels. The same peaks appear in the average energy distribution. There are three peaks. The one with the lowest energy of 0.19 is for populations consisting of agents with mostly two vowels, as systems with fewer vowels have inherently lower energy. The second peak, at energy 0.55, is for populations with agents that have three vowels, while the peak at energy 1.06 is for systems with four vowels.

The performance of the emerged systems will now be compared with that of random systems. Because these systems were not generated with an

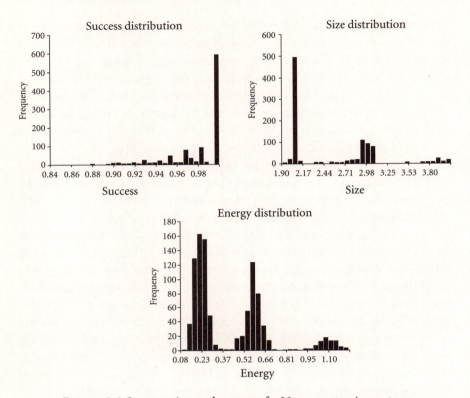

FIGURE 5.6. Success, size, and energy of a 20 per cent noise system

imitation game, the number of vowels was determined beforehand. It was chosen to investigate systems with three and with six vowels, because these correspond most closely to the systems that are found with 20 per cent and 10 per cent acoustic noise ψ_{ac}, respectively.

5.2.4 *Comparison with random systems*

The results of a simulation with random systems in which the agents have two or three vowels (as in the 20 per cent noise experiment) are shown in Figure 5.7. The results were obtained from calculating the energy and success of 1,000 populations of 20 randomly initialized agents. Note that the x-axis of the energy graph is logarithmic. This was necessary to accommodate the much higher values of the energy that were found. The average

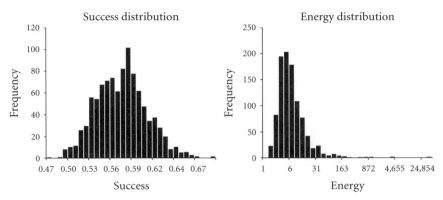

FIGURE 5.7. Success and energy of random systems with two or three vowels

of the average energy of the systems was 47, but the standard deviation of the energy was 1,102. The distribution is extremely skewed towards high energy values. In any case, it is clear that the energy of the random vowel systems is significantly higher than the energy of the vowel systems obtained by the simulation. The success values were calculated in a randomly initialized population of 20 agents with two or three vowels each (with the same distribution as in the simulations). Imitation games with 20 per cent noise added to the acoustic signals were played for all vowels of all agents, and the overall success was taken to be the ratio between the number of successful games and the total number of games. They have an average of 0.57 and a standard deviation of 0.035, which makes them significantly lower (at the 1 per cent level) than the success values of the systems obtained in the simulation. It can therefore be concluded that in the case of acoustic noise of 20 per cent the vowel systems are both more dispersed and more coherent than random.

The results for the random system with approximately five or six vowels per agent, as in the 10 per cent noise case, are presented in Figure 5.8. It can be seen that the success score of the random system is 0.51, with a standard deviation of 0.024. The energy of the emerged systems is extremely high, on average 112 with a standard deviation of 1,162. Again the energy distribution is very skewed, and therefore a logarithmic scale was used for displaying it. Apparently the average energy of the random systems is much higher than that of the systems obtained with the simulations. Also the success score of the random systems is significantly (at the 1 per cent level) lower than the success score of the vowel systems obtained in simulation.

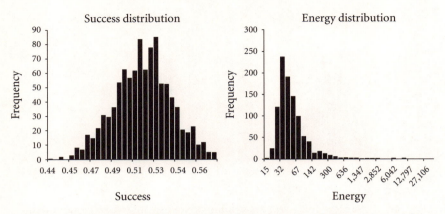

FIGURE 5.8. Success and energy of random systems with five or six vowels

The simulation with acoustic noise of 10 per cent therefore also performs better than random. But it is perhaps unexpected that the success score for random systems remains relatively high, above 0.50 in both cases. It can be shown by means of a mathematical argument that the success scores of random systems will not drop below 0.50.

5.2.5 *Comparison with optimal systems*

It appears that the imitation games result in systems that show better-than-random performance, something which could have been anticipated from an examination of the plot of the values of the obtained vowel systems. But how close do the vowel systems of the model come to the optimally dispersed vowel systems? A direct comparison of the results of the research into optimally dispersed systems (for example, that of Liljencrants and Lindblom 1972, of Vallée 1994, and of Schwartz, Boë, Vallée, and Abry 1997*b*) with the results obtained here is only possible in a qualitative, subjective way. The model used here differs in an important respect from the models researched elsewhere. In the work presented here, vowels are represented by their articulatory parameters and can only be optimized by shifting these articulatory parameters, while they are evaluated in acoustical space. In the other work, vowels were represented by their acoustic signals only, which could be directly manipulated in order to minimize the energy of the system.

The Liljencrants and Lindblom (1972) model was therefore reproduced, using articulatory representations for the vowels and using the synthesis function and perception function described in the previous chapter. The energy of the vowel systems was minimized by a gradient-descent method. First the system was initialized with vowels at random positions scattered throughout the articulatory space. Then for all vowels in the system in turn, it was calculated whether a small shift (either a decrease or an increase) in one of the three articulatory dimensions would reduce the total energy. If this was the case, the shift in vowel position was kept. If not, the vowel remained at its old position. This procedure was repeated until no more decrease in energy was possible. Note that the end result is not necessarily always the same vowel system. The system could become stuck in different (local) minima, depending on the initial conditions and on the sequence followed by the minimization procedure. This will be apparent from the figures.

The systems that resulted from running the minimization procedure with three vowel prototypes are presented in Figure 5.9. (This figure may be compared with Figure 5.21.) The most frequent of these systems (type 2) is the canonical three-vowel system with vowels [i], [a], and [u]. The less frequent type (type 1) is a 'vertical' vowel system consisting of [i], [e], and [a]. Although vowel systems of this particular composition probably do not appear in human languages, there are 'vertical' vowel systems with three elements, such as the Caucasian language Kabardian (Choi 1991, Ladefoged and Maddieson 1996, pp. 286–288), but these are usually more centralized: [ɨ], [ə], and [a] in the case of Kabardian. In cases like these, other factors, such as articulatory ease or historical processes, probably played a role.

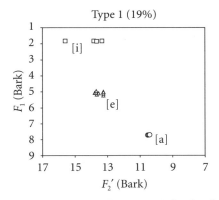
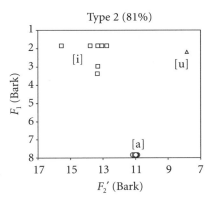

FIGURE 5.9. Optimal systems with three vowels

In any case, the most interesting part of these simulations is not the actual systems in which they result, but their energy. This is presented in Figure 5.10. It can be observed that there are several peaks in the energy graph. The highest peak is at energy 0.22. This peak corresponds to the most frequently occurring vowel systems. The peaks around energy levels 0.30–0.34 correspond to the vowel systems of type 2 that have front high vowels that are a little further back than [i], causing the somewhat dispersed cluster in the left plot of Figure 5.9. The peaks around 0.42–0.50 correspond to vowel systems of type 1. The clusters in the graph of this vowel system are slightly larger than those of type 2, so energies will occur in a larger range.

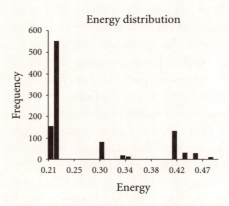

FIGURE 5.10. Energy of an optimal three-vowel system

The optimal systems with six vowels are presented in Figure 5.11. (This figure may be compared with Figure 5.24.) There is a greater number of different optimal systems for six vowels than there is for three. With the exception of type 4, all of these systems are realistic, and can be found in human languages. Type 4 is a typical example of a case where the minimization process became stuck at a local minimum, probably because the random initialization created too many vowels towards the front. The split of the high front vowel [i] that can be observed in almost all of these graphs is probably caused by the discontinuity of the perception function (described in the previous chapter).

From the data in Nathalie Vallée's thesis (Vallée 1994, Appendix 2), it is possible to identify languages that have systems of the types found in the simulations. An example of a language with a system like type 1 would

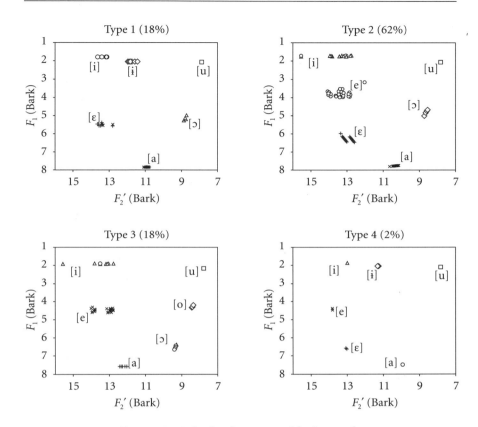

FIGURE 5.11. Optimal systems with six vowels

be Saami (Hasselbrink 1965), of a language of type 2 would be Chamorro (Seiden 1960), and of a language of type 3 would be Hakka (Hashimoto 1973). These types are not the most frequently occurring types of systems with six vowels in the world's languages, but they do agree quite well with the results Berrah (1998) obtained.

However, reproducing the most frequent vowel systems of the world's languages was not the aim of these simulations. The aim was to calculate the energies of (near-)optimal vowel systems that could be obtained with the synthesis and perception functions that are used in the imitation games. The energies that were obtained are given in Figure 5.12. The energy distribution has a large peak near 2.8, corresponding to the six-vowel systems of type 2 in Figure 5.11. The smaller peaks between 2.95 and 3.54 correspond to vowel systems of type 1 and type 3, respectively, while the two very small peaks around 3.94 correspond to the vowel systems of type 4.

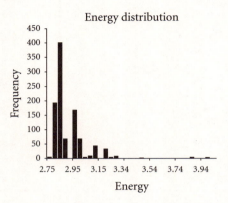

FIGURE 5.12. Energy of optimal six-vowel systems

5.2.6 *Conclusion of comparison*

The reason for calculating these optimal energies was to get an idea of how close to optimal the energies of the systems obtained through the imitation games are. The distribution of the average energies of the systems with acoustic noise $\psi_{ac} = 20\%$ can be found in Figure 5.6. Here there are peaks at 0.19 and 0.55, and the range is 0.08 to 1.14. This seems to be lower than the optimal energy, but note that there are also agents with only *two* vowels. In any case, these energy values compare very favourably with the optimal case, especially if one takes into account that the most frequent energies in the random systems were around 6.

The energies of systems with acoustic noise of 10 per cent can be found in Figure 5.5. Here there are peaks around energy values 4.38, 5.88, and 10.97 and the range is between 1.49 and 14.27. This also compares favourably with the energy values that were found in the optimal systems, although the systems seem to be somewhat further removed from the optimum. This is understandable, because there are many more possible configurations with five or six vowels than with only two or three.

The overall conclusion from this analysis is that the systems obtained from the imitation games compare favourably with optimal systems and are much better than random ones. They can therefore be assumed to be realistic. They enable successful imitation, because their success in imitation is much higher than in the case of random systems. However, one should not underestimate the success that can be obtained with random vowel systems, where the success rate tends towards 50 per cent for large numbers of vowels.

5.3 An articulatory view of the systems

So far all the systems have been shown in acoustic space. This was done because the agents have to distinguish vowels in acoustic space. The distribution in acoustic space is therefore the most relevant information for evaluating the quality of the emerging vowel systems. Moreover, the two-dimensional plot of the acoustic space is much easier to interpret than a three-dimensional projection of the articulatory parameters. However, it would be interesting to know whether the vowels also form clusters and whether they are also evenly distributed in articulatory space. This is not directly obvious. Acoustic space is two-dimensional (the first formant and the effective second formant), whereas articulatory space is three-dimensional. This means that many different possible articulations will map to the same acoustic signal. Vowel clusters in articulatory space could therefore be much more dispersed than vowel clusters in acoustic space.

This is illustrated in Figure 5.13. This figure shows a vowel system that was obtained with the default values for the parameters, after 25,000 imitation games in a population of 20 agents with the acoustic noise set to 20 per cent. This figure is an attempt to plot three-dimensional information on a two-dimensional plane. In the lower left corner is a perspective view of the three-dimensional system. The grey circles represent the agents' vowel prototypes. The projections of these prototypes in the rounding–position, the rounding–height, and the position-height planes are plotted as little dots on the walls of the diagram. These points can be considered 'shadows' of the vowel prototypes. For reference these planes are also plotted as flat squares around the perspective diagram. The same vowel system, but plotted in the acoustic space, is given in the left part of Figure 5.29.

It can be seen from Figure 5.13 that the clusters are quite concentrated in the position and height dimensions, but rather dispersed in the rounding dimension, with the exception of the cluster representing [u]. However, the clusters are well apart in the acoustic space as a whole, so they are easily kept apart. In a system of only three vowels it appears not to be necessary

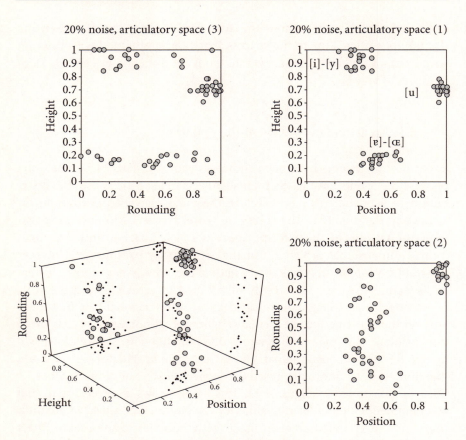

FIGURE 5.13. Articulatory representations of a 20 per cent noise system

to control all articulatory parameters equally precisely. One could say that there is considerable allophonic variation in the vowel systems of the agents in this population. The two parameters that are most carefully controlled are vowel position and height, as these influence the first and effective second formant most directly. Note, however, that in acoustic space the clusters are more compact than in any of the articulatory dimensions, reflecting the fact that the same signal can be achieved by different articulations.

In Figure 5.14, on the other hand, most of the clusters are much more compact. Just as in human vowel systems, back vowels are rounded. The only exception to this is the low back vowel, which is also often unrounded in human languages. The high and low front vowels of the agents are unrounded as well, which agrees with the observation that front vowels are usually unrounded in human languages. Apparently there is an emergent rule: [±**front**] → [∓**rounded**]. However, the mid front vowel is rounded (with for three agents the schwa [ə] as allophone). The high central vowel is rounded for some agents and unrounded for others, without any intermediate values. However, if one looks at the acoustic realization of this vowel (shown in the right part of Figure 5.29) one finds only one compact cluster. Apparently the acoustic realizations of the two different articulations are almost the same. This was to be expected, because the acoustic space is two-dimensional and the articulatory space is three-dimensional. But this

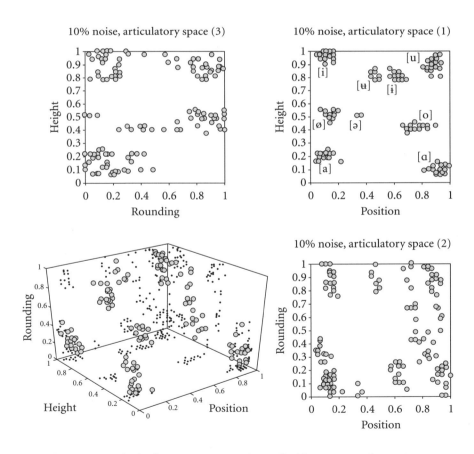

FIGURE 5.14. Articulatory representations of a 10 per cent noise system

phenomenon is not limited to the artificial system. Humans, too, are able to produce the same sound with different articulatory settings (see, for example, Lindblom 1972, Maeda 1989).

The articulatory view of the emerging vowel systems shows that, even though articulatory constraints hardly play a role in the success of the imitation games, compact clusters do form in the articulatory space. Also, the articulatory parameters of the vowels in the agents' repertoires are comparable to the ones of the vowels in human systems, with, for example, rounded back vowels and unrounded front vowels (although this is not always the case). But it can be concluded that not only the distribution in acoustic space of the emerging vowel systems is natural, but also their distribution in articulatory space.

5.4 Variable populations

According to Steels's theory of language as an adaptive system (Steels 1997*b*, Steels 1998*a*, Steels 1999) a language should be an open system. A language should be able to accommodate linguistic innovation, but it should also continue to exist despite changes of the population. It has already been shown that the simulation presented in the previous chapter is able to generate successful vowel systems from scratch. Also, agents can introduce new vowels into their vowel repertoires. If these vowels can easily be distinguished from the other, already existing vowels, all agents in the population will quickly adopt them. So it is clear that the 'language' (consisting of the vowel systems) of the agents is an open system as regards changes in the 'language' itself. However, it remains to be shown whether it is also an open system with respect to changes of the population. In research within the same theoretical framework, but directed towards different aspects of language, such as lexicon and semantics, simulations have shown that changes in population (within certain limits) do not influence the 'language' very much (Steels and Kaplan 1997, Kaplan 1998).

5.4.1 *Definition of measures and parameters of population change*

In order to investigate this, changes in the population should be made possible. This means that it must be possible to add new agents and to remove old ones. There are several ways to do this, but the simplest and most realistic way, and the one least likely to introduce artefacts, is to do it stochastically. Two probabilities are introduced: the probability p_b of a new agent being 'born' into the population and the probability p_d of an agent dying. Using a stochastic scheme for changing the population is less likely to introduce artefacts than any scheme based on regular replacement of the population (for example, replacing agents after a fixed number of time steps). Regularities are always arbitrary and might interfere in unknown ways with the imitation games. Stochastic replacement is also most realistic, because in human populations, too, birth and death are stochastic phenomena that cannot be predicted. However, one *can* make good predictions of the average rates of birth and death. These average rates are determined by the two probabilities.

The birth and death of agents take place with probabilities p_b and p_d in every imitation game. For a stable population size, on average p_b should be equal to p_d. A number of derived, 'demographic' measures are useful for describing population changes. These are the excess of births over deaths, or the growth of the population—which is defined as the expected number of agents that is added to the population per language game (that is, the difference between the probability of birth and the probability of death). The flux, or replacement rate of the population, is the number of agents that is expected to change during an imitation game and is defined as the sum of the probability of birth and the probability of death. The life expectancy of an agent is the average number of imitation games during which it is expected to stay in the population ($1/p_d$) and the half-life of a population is the expected number of imitation games that have to be played before half of the agents in the original population have been replaced. This is harder to calculate in the general case, so only estimates will be given.

5.4.2 *Maintaining a vowel system*

The first experiment to be done checks whether a vowel system that has emerged in a population that does *not* change can be maintained in a population that *does* change. The population size is 50 agents and the acoustic noise ψ_{ac} is set to 10 per cent. The population size is larger than in the experiments in the previous chapter, because the birth and death of new agents make the population size fluctuate. Fluctuations in a population of 20 agents might easily make the population too small, whereas fluctuations in a population of 50 agents have a much smaller relative influence. The results are shown in Figure 5.15. First the simulation is run for 25,000 imitation games in order to generate a vowel system that is almost fully developed. Then the probability of birth and death is set to 0.01. Thus the growth of the population is zero, the flux is 0.02, the life expectancy of an agent is 100 games, and the half-life of the population is approximately 3,500 imitation games. Figure 5.15 shows snapshots of the vowel systems of all the agents in the population at intervals of 5,000 games. In the frame on the bottom right, 15,000 imitation games have been played since the first frame, meaning that only 5 per cent of the agents in the original population are expected to be present. The population size is not completely stable. The original population consisted of 50 agents. In the second frame this has become 63, in the third 58, and in the last 42. It is clear that the original vowel system is not preserved in the changing

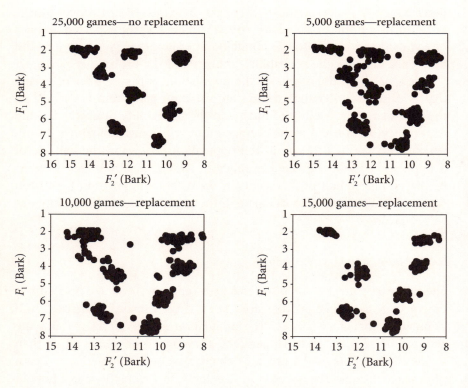

FIGURE 5.15. Vowel systems of imitation games with population replacement

population. On the other hand, the vowel system in Figure 5.15 does not change completely randomly either. It appears that the vowel systems that emerge from the stable population are too crowded for the changing population. A number of vowel clusters merge, there is a brief period of chaos, and then a new stable system emerges. Still, it remains true that this vowel system is less stable and successful than the vowel system in a population that does not change.

A number of variations of this experiment can be imagined by changing the rates of birth and death. The results of the previous experiment suggested that the vowel systems of changing populations converge to configurations with fewer vowel clusters than those in populations that do not change. Figure 5.16 illustrates the exploration of the long-term behaviour of vowel systems in populations that change at different rates. The frame on the top left shows the vowel system with which the populations started,

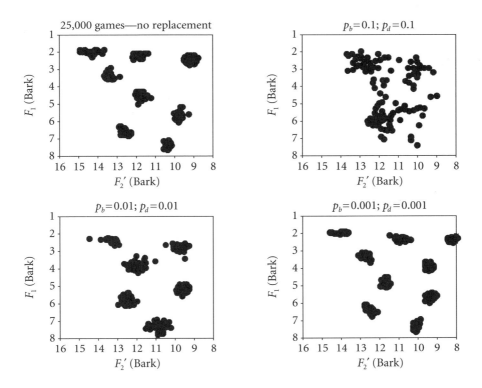

FIGURE 5.16. Vowel systems after complete population replacement

which is in fact the same system as that with which the simulation in Figure 5.15 started. The second frame shows the vowel systems of a population with rates of birth and death of 0.1 after 2,500 imitation games. In this case the half-life is approximately 340 games, so that less than 1 per cent of the original population is expected to be present. The third frame shows the vowel systems of a population with birth and death rates of 0.01 (effectively the same settings as in Figure 5.15) after 25,000 imitation games. The last frame shows the systems of a population with birth and death rates of 0.001 (half-life 35,000) after 250,000 imitation games. The population sizes have not remained completely constant. The population has increased to 59 in the second frame and to 81 in the third, and in the fourth has decreased to 43. It is obvious that although each of the populations has undergone approximately the same number of replacements, the system with the highest replacement rate becomes the most chaotic, while the system with the lowest replacement rate remains most stable. This is to be expected, as new agents in populations with lower replacement rates have more time to get used to the vowel systems of the other agents. Apparently agents in a population with a replacement rate of 0.2 only have time to learn two or three vowels (the number of clusters in the graph of the population's vowel systems). Agents in a population with flux of 0.02 have time to learn six vowels and agents in a population with flux of 0.002 have time to learn the maximum number of vowels that is stable in an unchanging population with the same parameter settings.

Table 5.1 shows the average success values, energies, and inventory sizes over 100 runs of the simulation for these three parameter settings, all starting with the vowel system given in the frame at the top left in Figure 5.16. They are given with their standard deviations. It should always be borne in mind that the distributions, especially that of energy, are not normal. When this table is compared with the results given in the previous chapter, it becomes clear that vowel systems in a changing population have less suc-

TABLE 5.1. Statistics of changing populations

	Flux 0.2, 1,500 games	Flux 0.02, 15,000 games	Flux 0.002, 150,000 games
Success	0.8117 ± 0.032	0.7675 ± 0.035	0.8375 ± 0.043
Energy	0.40 ± 0.79	2.84 ± 2.42	7.00 ± 3.34
Size	1.88 ± 1.03	4.55 ± 1.67	7.02 ± 1.34

cess than vowel systems in an unchanging population. From these results it can be determined that the final number of vowels is significantly (using the Kolmogorov–Smirnov test) lower for higher population fluxes than for lower ones.

5.4.3 *Emergence of a vowel system*

Stable vowel systems can be maintained in populations that change, even though the number of vowel prototypes might be smaller than in populations that do not change. The question now arises whether a vowel system could also emerge from scratch in a population that changes. It was shown in the previous section that vowel systems did emerge from scratch in a stable population. In the data presented so far in this chapter, it has been shown that the same mechanism that was responsible for the emergence of the vowel systems in the unchanging populations could also be used by new agents to learn an existing vowel system. If it is shown that the same mechanism can be used for making a vowel system emerge in a changing population, this supports Steels's hypothesis (Steels 1997*b*, Steels 1998*a*) that the same mechanisms that are responsible for learning language could be responsible for the emergence of a new language.

Figure 5.17 shows the results of such an experiment. In this figure, which can be compared with Figure 5.1, the emergence of a coherent and realistic vowel system can be observed. The frames show the vowel systems of the population of 50 agents after 1,000, 2,000, 5,000, 10,000, and 20,000 imitation games. The probability of birth and death was set to 0.01. The half-life of the population is then 3,500 games, implying that after 20,000 imitation games on average only one agent of the original population is expected to remain. The number of agents in the populations shown in the frames was 59, 62, 67, 66, and 64, respectively. Two differences between Figure 5.17 and Figure 5.1 are noteworthy. The first is that larger clusters emerge and these will generally be fewer in number. This is in line with the findings of the experiments presented above. The second difference is that the emergence of the vowel system occurs much more slowly than in the unchanging population. It appears that the movement of agents entering and leaving the population makes it harder for a common vowel system to be accepted by all agents.

These results show that the imitation game truly is an open system, both with respect to the language itself and with respect to the population of

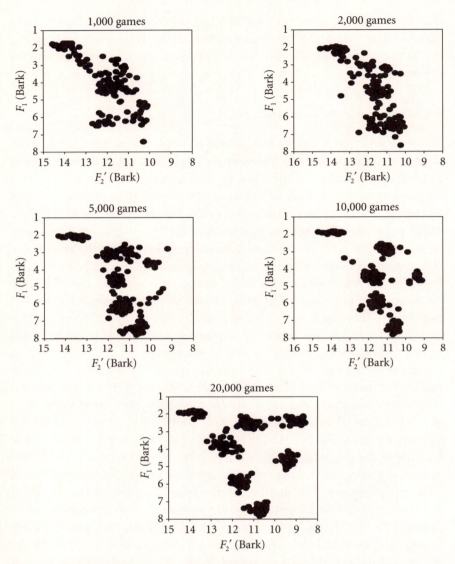

FIGURE 5.17. Emergence of a vowel system in a changing population

speakers. Even though both the language and the population of speakers are highly dynamic, a stable (and realistic) system of sounds for successful imitation emerges.

5.4.4 *Age structure*

It is unfortunate, however, that in populations that change, not so many vowel clusters can be maintained as in systems in an unchanging population. Decreasing noise levels, or decreasing the step size ε with which vowel prototypes are improved, would increase the number of vowel prototypes, but in unchanging populations with the same parameter settings, the number of vowel prototypes would be higher still. There is one case, however, where changing populations can maintain more vowel prototypes than unchanging ones. This is the case where the number of times an agent can improve a vowel prototype (the number of *practice steps*) is limited. It was found that if the number of practice steps was limited in unchanging populations, there would be an intermediate step size with which vowel prototypes could be moved towards perceived goals where the number of vowels would be highest. In the case of the changing population, an age structure can be introduced in which young agents have a large step size, so they can imitate new vowels relatively quickly, while older agents have a smaller step size, so they provide a stable target for the younger agents.

An example of the result of an experiment with such a model is shown in Figure 5.18. In this figure the vowel systems of four populations are shown. Each of these populations consisted of 50 agents initially and was initialized with the same vowel system. The initial vowel system is shown as open squares in the graph. All populations were run for 15,000 imitation games, with different parameter settings, and the resulting vowel systems are plotted as black circles. All parameters were set to their default values, acoustic noise was 10 per cent, the probability of birth and death was 0.01. The maximum number of practice steps for all agents was limited to 10. The upper left and lower right frames show the results of populations where there was no age structure. In the upper left frame, a population is shown which had a practice step size of 0.01. As can be seen from the frame, the number of vowel clusters after 15,000 games is much lower than in the original system. Clearly, the younger agents have not been able to learn the older agents' vowels. In the lower right frame, the practice step size was set to 0.03. Here the number of clusters has remained about the same, but they have become bigger and slightly more diffuse.

The other two frames show systems that resulted from agents that were in between the agents from the upper left and lower right frames. These

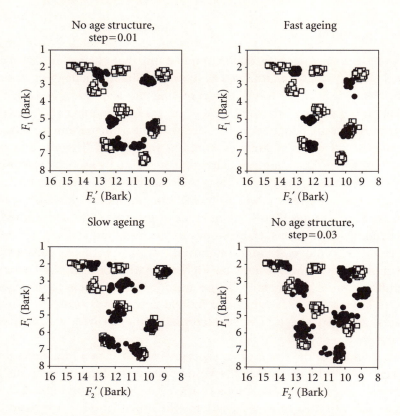

FIGURE 5.18. Influence of age structure on transfer of vowel systems

agents changed their practice step size from 0.03 to 0.01 over their lifetime, using the following mechanism:

$$\varepsilon_t = \varepsilon_{t-1} + \alpha_{ageing}(\varepsilon_\infty - \varepsilon_{t-1}), \tag{5.3}$$

where ε_t is the practice step size at time t, ε_∞ is the final step size of old agents (set to 0.01 in these experiments) and α_{ageing} is the speed with which the agents age. The population in the upper right and that in the lower left differ in their values for α_{ageing}. The first one has $\alpha_{ageing} = 0.1$, causing agents to age quickly, and the second one has $\alpha_{ageing} = 0.01$, causing agents to age slowly.

Statistics of simulations with parameter settings corresponding to these figures are presented in Table 5.2. The sequence of the columns corresponds to the sequence of the frames in Figure 5.18. The table shows the averages of success, energy, size, and similarity over 100 runs of each of the simulations, consisting of 15,000 imitation games, every time starting with the same population of 50 agents that was used as a starting point in all previous experiments. Also shown are the standard deviations. The *similarity* is a new measure, and illustrates the difference between the present system and the system with which the agents started. It is calculated by playing 1,000 imitation games (without updates of the vowel inventories) with a random agent of the original population as initiator and a random agent from the present population as imitator and 1,000 imitation games with the roles reversed. The average success over these 2,000 games is then taken as the similarity.

The most interesting measures for assessing how well the original vowel system has been preserved are those of size and similarity. The original system contained eight vowels, so none of the populations preserves it completely, as they all end up with (on average) fewer vowels. The sizes of vowel systems of the two populations with an age structure are significantly greater than those of the populations without an age structure according to the Kolmogorov–Smirnov test. This test does not find a significant difference in inventory size *between* the two populations with an age structure. It does find a significant difference (at the 1 per cent level) between the energies of the systems, with the slowly ageing population having lowest energy on average. Comparing the similarities of the populations with and without an age structure, it is found that the ones with an age structure have significantly higher similarity (at the 1 per cent level) than the ones without an age structure. It can therefore be concluded that populations with an age structure preserve the vowel systems better when the number of practice steps is limited.

TABLE 5.2. Statistics of populations with and without an age structure

Population	$\varepsilon_0 = 0.01$ $\varepsilon_\infty = 0.01$ $\alpha_{ageing} = 0$	$\varepsilon_0 = 0.03$ $\varepsilon_\infty = 0.01$ $\alpha_{ageing} = 0.1$	$\varepsilon_0 = 0.03$ $\varepsilon_\infty = 0.01$ $\alpha_{ageing} = 0.01$	$\varepsilon_0 = 0.03$ $\varepsilon_\infty = 0.03$ $\alpha_{ageing} = 0$
Success	0.8531 ± 0.040	0.7701 ± 0.035	0.7930 ± 0.041	0.8041 ± 0.041
Energy	4.04 ± 0.59	5.55 ± 1.10	5.10 ± 0.95	3.83 ± 0.72
Size	4.77 ± 0.40	5.66 ± 0.63	5.61 ± 0.58	5.14 ± 0.50
Similarity	0.7347 ± 0.023	0.8231 ± 0.028	0.8235 ± 0.032	0.7884 ± 0.032

Many more experiments can be conceived with dynamic populations. However, they are beyond the scope of this book. The experiments shown in this section are just an illustration of the possibilities of a fast population-based simulation of linguistic phenomena.

5.5 Human vowel system universals and typology

In the discussion so far, only indirect or impressionistic comparisons have been made with human vowel systems. This section and the next present a more detailed investigation of the similarity between vowel systems that emerge from the simulations and real human vowel systems. In order to understand the relationship between the two systems some knowledge of the universals and the typology of human vowel systems is required. Universals have already been discussed in a general way in Chapter 2. This section presents a more detailed and concrete overview of typology and universals, and discusses what predictions a theory that claims to model the emergence of vowel systems should make. This discussion provides an introduction to the next section, in which the different vowel systems that emerge from the simulation are compared with data on human vowel systems, and it is verified whether the frequency with which different systems emerge is comparable to the frequency with which similar systems are found in human languages.

It was noted in Chapter 2 that human sound systems, and more specifically human vowel systems, show a number of remarkable regularities. Humans are able to distinguish a huge number of different vowel sounds *in principle*. According to Ladefoged and Maddieson (1996) there are languages that make five distinctions in the height of vowels, languages that make three distinctions in their position, and languages that make three distinctions in lip rounding. This would make for a total of at least 45 possible basic vowel qualities. However, any one human language uses only a very limited subset of these. Vallée (1994), who investigated the UPSID$_{317}$, found that the maximum number of different vowel qualities that are used in any language in the sample is 15, in Norwegian (Vanvik 1972). There are languages that have more vowel phonemes, but these will use other processes, such as length, nasalization, and pharyngealization, not quality, in order to distinguish vowels. Furthermore, the small subsets of the possible vowels that languages use are not chosen at random (see Crothers 1978, section 4.5, for a discussion of randomness in relation to five-vowel systems). Some vowels appear more often than others and vowel systems tend to be quite symmetrical. Typologies of possible human vowel systems have been based on these observations.

5.5.1 *The basis of typologies of human vowel systems*

Before we embark on a description of the proposed typologies of human vowel systems, the precise basis of these typologies needs to be clarified. They are based on phonetic descriptions of the vowel phonemes of languages. Phonemes are by definition minimal units of sound that can make a difference in meaning. However, it is quite possible that two speech sounds that are different (but close) phonetically do not make any distinction in meaning. These sounds are then called allophones of a phoneme. This happens, for example, through the influence exerted by neighbouring sounds. A description of the phonemes of a language necessarily abstracts from this allophonic variation. If one wishes to describe a language this is not a problem. On the other hand, if one wishes to classify languages on the basis of which phonetic signals are used for realizing their vowel phonemes it does become a problem. A choice needs to be made as to which phonetic realization is representative of the phoneme. Usually the most frequent allophone of a phoneme is taken to be the representative one. These representative allophones can then serve as a basis for a typology of possible vowel systems. Some researchers have even considered vowel systems with phonetically different elements as belonging to the same category (for example Crothers 1978, who analyses [i], [a], [u] and [i], [a], [o] as belonging to the same type).

It will be assumed here that this is a valid methodology. However, it should be kept in mind that a typology and classification of vowel systems is based in the first place on abstract phonemes. The actual observed signals in a language can be considerably more messy than would be expected from the typological classification of the language. A case in point is the vowel system of English. In Figure 5.19 it is given as: [i], [ɪ], [ɛ], [æ], [ɑ], [ɔ], [ʊ], [u], [ɜ], and [ʌ]. This seems like a reasonably symmetrical ten-vowel system with two central vowels. But an examination of the figure shows that the actual clusters (which are based on data from many different

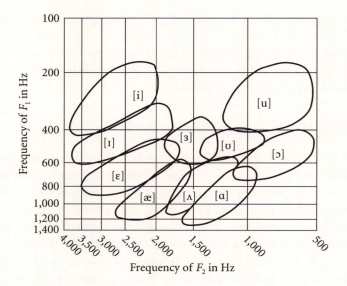

FIGURE 5.19. Vowels in English

Note: The axes in this figure have been changed from those in the source in order to make the figure more comparable with the figures of the artificial systems presented in this book. Only the outlines of the clusters have been retained; the individual data points have been removed.

Source: Based on data in Rabiner and Schafer (1978: fig. 3.4), itself derived from Peterson and Barney (1952).

speakers) cover quite a considerable area of the acoustic space, meaning that the vowels could have been labelled differently as well. Also, there seems to be overlap between the different vowel clusters, indicating that it is not always possible to say to which phoneme a given signal would have to be mapped. (However, it is probable that this overlap disappears if higher formants are also taken into account.)

The conclusion therefore is that one should not always expect the actual observed sounds of a human language to follow a given typology. Typologies are based on data that are to at least some extent abstract and idealized. Vowel systems that emerge from a simulation should therefore not be expected to follow the typology exactly. They should rather be expected to follow it in a general way so that the same symmetries and the same number of distinctions in height and position appear. However, they do not necessarily have to consist of exactly the vowels predicted by the typology.

5.5.2 *Classification and typology of human vowel systems*

Having given this warning, we now introduce the classification of vowel systems developed by a large number of researchers. Soon after the idea of the phoneme was introduced, Trubetzkoy (1929) attempted to classify the vowel systems of the world's languages. This classification was elaborated upon by others (Hockett 1955, Sedlak 1969), and has been used to construct a typology of vowel systems together with a number of universals (Crothers 1978, Vallée 1994, Ladefoged and Maddieson 1996, Schwartz, Boë, and Vallée 1997). Since the 1970s explanations of the universal tendencies have been investigated with computer models based on functional criteria (see, for example, Liljencrants and Lindblom 1972, Schwartz, Boë, Vallée, and Abry 1997*b*). These models are discussed briefly in Chapter 2.

Here, we mainly follow Crothers's (1978) typology. This typology is based on the Stanford Phonology Archive (Vihman 1976), the predecessor of UPSID, which consisted of 209 languages, and is therefore reasonably representative. An advantage of the typology for use in the research presented in this book is that it classifies the vowels in acoustic space. This agrees with the way similarities between vowels are evaluated in the simulations presented in the previous chapters. It also ignores other articulatory parameters that might be used for distinguishing vowels, such as length, nasalization, and pharyngealization. These parameters cannot be used by the agents in the simulations, so they should not be used in evaluating the realism of the emerging systems either. More recent work on the typology of vowel systems (Vallée 1994, Schwartz, Boë, and Vallée 1997) does take these distinctions into account and is therefore less applicable to the work at hand.

Crothers's typology is based on acoustic distinctions in the F_1–F_2 space. As rounding and tongue position both have the effect of changing the second formant, they are considered as one parameter, rather than two. This allows Crothers to lump together most central vowels, without taking into account whether the acoustic signals are produced through lip rounding or through centralizing the tongue position. The vowel systems /i, e, a, o, u, i/ and /i, e, a, o, u, y/ would thus be analysed as belonging to the same type. Whether this is sound practice when classifying actual human languages is questionable. Schwartz, Boë, and Vallée (1997), for example, do make distinctions between the different central vowels. However, the acoustic representation of the vowels in the simulations does not make a distinction between different central vowels, so Crothers's (1978) typology is quite well suited for comparing human languages with the outcomes of the simulations.

In general, Crothers seems to be more interested in the relation between the different positions of the vowel phonemes than in their absolute positions. For example, he classifies vowel systems /i, a, u/, /i, a, ɯ/, /i, a, o/, etc. as the same triangular three-vowel system /i, a, u/. This is acceptable as long as one is interested in *classifying* vowel systems obtained from either a description of a language or a computer simulation. This is what will be done in the next section. However, when lumping vowels together like this, one should be very careful about making inferences in the other direction, such as: 'There are no languages without [i], [a], and [u]'.

A third simplification of the vowel systems in his sample that Crothers makes is in the way he handles other articulatory parameters besides height, position, and lip rounding. If other parameters are used, Crothers counts vowels that have different settings for this parameter, and that are very close (but not always equal) in quality, as representing only one vowel quality in the system. For example, he analyses the vowel system of German, consisting of /ɪ, ɛ, ʏ, œ, ɐ, ʊ, ɔ, iː, eː, yː, øː, aː, uː, oː/, as a symmetrical seven-vowel system with two central vowels. Again, this might not be the best approach for dealing with human languages. In their classification, Schwartz, Boë, and Vallée (1997) analyse German as a system with 16 different vowel qualities (they also count /ə/ and /ɛː/ as phonemes). However, although it is true that length (or other) distinctions are often accompanied by quality distinctions, the length gives an extra cue for recognizing the vowels. Vowel systems that do make length (or other secondary) distinctions could therefore possibly be slightly more crowded than vowel systems in which length distinctions are not made. As the agents are not able to make such distinctions, it is probably not fair to try to fit their vowel systems into a typology that is based on possibly slightly more crowded vowel systems that *are* using extra distinctions.

The best way to illustrate Crothers's (1978) observations on vowel systems is with the diagram presented in Figure 5.20. This diagram shows the sequence of vowels used by differently sized vowel systems of the world's languages. It should be interpreted as follows. If a vowel system has three vowels, it consists of /i, a, u/ or at least it has vowels that are near these three centres. If it has four vowels, it adds either /ɨ/ or /ɛ/. For systems with five and more vowels, one can just follow the arrows down, until one reaches the maximum size of eight or nine vowels. Although Crothers notes that there are exceptions to this hierarchy, the great majority of languages follow it. But, as has been mentioned above, Crothers allows considerable slack in the assignment of phonetic symbols to the phonemes of a language, so that his hierarchy says more about the relative positions of the vowels in the systems than about their actual precise phonetic value. However, Vallée (1994, p. 94), who uses a different sample of languages (UPSID$_{317}$) and a different methodology, comes to a rather similar hierarchy, although the order of appearance of the central vowels is different.

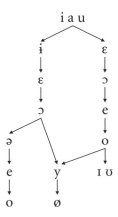

FIGURE 5.20. Vowel system hierarchy according to Crothers
Source: Crothers (1978).

Crothers also summarizes his observations in a number of rules, the first 12 of which (Crothers 1978, Appendix I) are quoted below:

1. All languages have /i a u/.
2. All languages with four or more vowels have /ɨ/ or /ɛ/.
3. Languages with five or more vowels have /ɛ/. They generally also have /ɔ/.
4. Languages with six or more vowels have /ɔ/ and also either /ɨ/ or /e/, generally the former.
5. Languages with seven or more vowels have /e o/ or /ɨ ə/. (The types /ɨ ə/ may be represented by /ü ö/.)
6. Languages with eight or more vowels have /e/.
7. Languages with nine or more vowels generally have /o/.
8. A contrast between five basic vowel qualities is the norm for human language, and in general, the most common systems are those with close to this number of basic vowels.

9. The number of height distinctions in a system is typically equal to or greater than the number of backness distinctions.
10. Languages with two or more interior vowels always have a high one.
11. The number of vowels in a column of interior vowels cannot exceed the number in the front or back columns.
12. The number of height distinctions in front vowels is equal to or greater than the number in back vowels.

Rules 13, 14, and 15 have to do with vowel length and nasalization, so they are not relevant for the present purposes. Note also that Crothers uses the American notation /ü ö/ for front rounded vowels, instead of the IPA notation /y ø/.

5.5.3 *Conformity of emerged and real languages to the typology*

If the simulations presented in this book are realistic, the vowel systems that emerge should conform to these rules, and to the hierarchy of Figure 5.20. The extent of conformity is investigated in the next section. However, it should be kept in mind that actual languages diverge from the typology, usually in detail, but sometimes completely. One could say that the vowel systems of languages conform to the typology and universals with a high probability. One should make a distinction between investigating which functional criteria play a role in determining the shape of vowel systems, and actually predicting the vowel systems that appear in the world's languages. Optimizing an artificial vowel system according to criteria of acoustic dispersion, as was done, for example, by Liljencrants and Lindblom (1972), is good for testing whether acoustic distance plays a role in determining the shape of human vowel systems. As vowel systems that are (near-)optimal with respect to acoustic dispersion appear significantly more often than sub-optimal ones, it clearly plays a role. Such models are not complete, however, for actually predicting the vowel systems that do occur in human languages, as they will tend to produce only optimal systems, whereas non-optimal systems appear as well, albeit with lower frequency.

Any model that claims to predict the vowel systems of languages should not only predict the vowel systems that are observed most often, but also, with a lower probability, the systems that appear less frequently. The frequency distribution of the predicted systems should conform to the frequency distribution of human vowel systems. Models that work with populations of agents, as opposed to models that simply optimize, should certainly do this, because they investigate not only which factors play a role in determining the shape of vowel systems, but actually how these factors are implemented as well. This is a weak point in the work of Berrah (1998), whose model mostly predicts the most frequently occurring systems.

The vowel systems that emerge from an agent simulation should therefore conform with human languages not only in terms of their vowel inventories, but also in the frequency distributions of the different types of systems.

5.6 Relation between systems that emerge from simulations and real systems

An attempt is now made to construct a typology of the vowel systems that emerge from the simulations to mirror the typology that exists for human vowel systems. For this a number of simulation trials with different parameter settings have been run in order to generate a large number of stable artificial vowel systems. Each parameter setting resulted in vowel systems with a number of vowels in a limited range. These systems were classified in the same way as the systems of Crothers (1978) were classified. That is to say, more attention was paid to the relative arrangement of the vowel prototypes than to their exact phonetic values. A check was then carried out to ascertain whether the types of vowel systems that emerged and their relative frequencies were comparable to Crothers's results. The parameter values were changed so that systems with different numbers of vowels emerged. The systems that emerged were compared and classified and a further check was carried out to see whether the same hierarchy of appearance of vowels in systems of different sizes was found in the simulations as in real languages.

5.6.1 *Three-vowel systems*

The first vowel systems discussed were obtained from the vowel simulation with the standard parameter settings, with a population of 20 agents and with acoustic noise set to 18 per cent. The simulation was run 100 times. For each run 25,000 imitation games were played. From each of the resulting populations, the average number of vowels per agent was calculated.

Then one of the agents that had a number of vowels that was equal to the average was selected, and its vowel system was classified. This was done on the basis of the number of front, back, and central vowels, and on the basis of whether the vowel system had one or two low vowels. This did not play a very important role in the trials with 18 per cent noise, because only systems with three or four vowels emerged. There were 32 systems with, on average, three vowel prototypes, and 68 systems with, on average, four vowel prototypes. These numbers should not be compared with the frequencies of three- and four-vowel systems, respectively, in human languages, because it is possible, by changing the noise parameter, to ensure the relative abundance of systems with any number of vowels.

The three-vowel systems that emerged are shown in Figure 5.21. Again, the acoustic prototypes of the agents' vowels are shown in acoustic space on the basis of the first and effective second formant frequencies on the logarithmic Bark scale. Although the points plotted look very much like those of vowel systems shown in earlier figures in this chapter, they actually show something quite different. The points plotted in previous diagrams showed the vowel prototypes of all the agents in *one* population. The clusters in those diagrams corresponded with the vowel prototypes that were recognized by all agents in that population. The diagrams in Figure 5.21, however, show the vowel systems of agents from *different* populations, classified in each diagram on the basis of the shape of each individual agent's vowel system. The individual agents' vowel systems are taken to be representative of the population from which they were taken. Whereas in the previous diagrams in this chapter all the agents shown had played

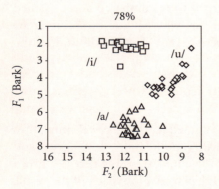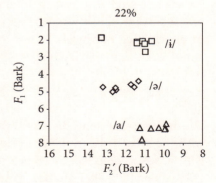

FIGURE 5.21. Classification of three-vowel systems

imitation games with each other, in Figure 5.21 (and other diagrams of classifications in this chapter) none of the agents have played imitation games with each other. The similarities between their vowel systems are therefore due not to their interactions, but to the fact that populations have been attracted towards similar vowel systems. The lack of interaction between the agents also accounts for the larger size of the clusters and their greater degree of overlap.

The 32 vowel systems with three vowels can be classified into two types: one that is roughly triangular and one that is roughly vertical. The first type appears in 78 per cent of the cases and the second type appears in 22 per cent of the cases. This is not quite the same distribution as in human languages. The first of Crothers's (1978) universals says that all languages have /i, a, u/. However, here about one-fifth of the emerging three-vowel systems are vertical and, although vertical systems do appear in human languages (Choi 1991, Ladefoged and Maddieson 1996), they are quite rare. Also, the triangular vowel systems have a mid back vowel [o] instead of a high back vowel [u]. Most probably this has to do with the position of the high front vowel, which appears to be consistently too far back, so that there is more distance between it and a mid back vowel than a high back vowel. This seems to be a problem with the synthesis and perception functions, which was also observed in Figures 5.9 and 5.10. It seems that although it is possible for the agents to produce and perceive high and front vowels, in practice it is almost impossible to learn this vowel, or to reach it through optimizations, as in Figures 5.9 and 5.10.

5.6.2 *Four-vowel systems*

The situation with four-vowel systems is much more realistic. The four-vowel systems were taken from the simulation with acoustic noise of 15 per cent. The other parameters were set to the same values as in the previous experiment. From this run, 51 systems with four vowels and 49 systems with five vowels emerged. The classification of four-vowel systems is shown in Figure 5.22. This shows that all the four-vowel systems that were found did contain /i, a, u/, thus conforming to Crothers's first universal. About 55 per cent of the systems contain a mid central vowel, and about 45 per cent of the systems contain a mid front vowel. Although Crothers's (1978) second universal says that all languages with four or more vowels have either /ɨ/ or /ɛ/, and the four-vowel systems with a central vowel that

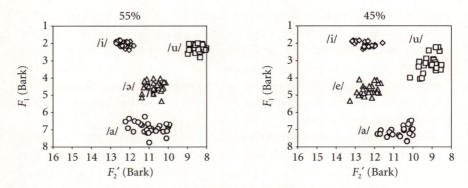

FIGURE 5.22. Classification of four-vowel systems

emerged have /ə/ instead, they still conform quite closely to Crothers's universals. The discrepancy is again probably due to the fact that the high front vowel is quite far to the back, so that there is not sufficient room for a high central vowel. If the results are compared with Schwartz, Boë, and Vallée (1997) it is found that, in their data, systems without central vowels occur much more frequently than systems with central vowels, whereas in the simulation they occur in roughly equal proportions.

5.6.3 *Five-vowel systems*

Five-vowel systems are shown in Figure 5.23. The vowel systems were obtained from the same simulation, with 15 per cent acoustic noise, as the four-vowel systems. Here the resulting classification corresponds well with human sound systems. Of the 49 systems, 88 per cent consisted of the symmetrical five-vowel system. Eight per cent have a central vowel and two front vowels, while 4 per cent have a central vowel and two back vowels. The most frequent type conforms to Crothers's first three universals. The type that occurs in 8 per cent of the cases conforms to the first two universals, and the type that occurs in 4 per cent of the cases only to the first universal. Schwartz, Boë, and Vallée (1997) found that the type at the top left in Figure 5.23 occurs in 89 per cent of the languages with five vowels in UPSID$_{317}$. They found that systems with a central vowel have more front vowels or more back vowels equally often (in 5 per cent of the cases). The results of the simulation with five-vowel systems therefore correspond very well with what is found in human languages.

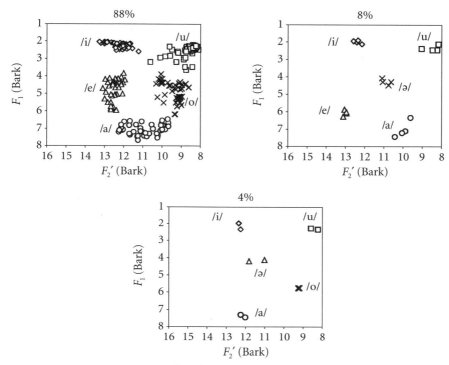

FIGURE 5.23. Classification of five-vowel systems

5.6.4 *Six-vowel systems*

Systems with six vowels were obtained from a run with the acoustic noise parameter ψ_{ac} set to 12 per cent. The rest of the parameters were exactly as in the previous experiments. From the 100 runs that were made, 54 resulted in vowel systems with six prototypes. The resulting classes of systems are shown in Figure 5.24. There are more types in this figure than in the previous figure, because the bigger a system becomes, the more ways there are to distribute the vowel prototypes. For this reason the different types in this figure have been assigned letters in order to facilitate reference to them. Type A is the most frequent type, occurring in 55 per cent of the cases. It consists of the symmetrical five-vowel system with a more or less high central vowel. This system conforms to Crothers's first four universals, as do types B and C (for a total of 86 per cent of the systems). Type F lacks /ɔ/, thus violating universal 4. Type E is quite similar

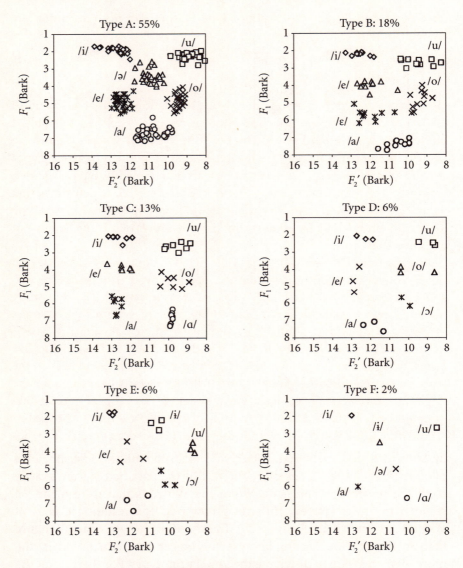

FIGURE 5.24. Classification of six-vowel systems

to type A, except that the back vowels are lower. The systems also compare favourably with the results of Schwartz, Boë, and Vallée (1997). For the 60 six-vowel systems they found in UPSID$_{317}$, 43 per cent were of type A, 20 per cent were of type B, 5 per cent were of type C, 7 per cent were of type D, and 20 per cent were of type E. They did not encounter any systems of type F.

5.6.5 *Seven-vowel systems*

Seven-vowel systems were obtained from simulations with acoustic noise of 10 per cent. From the 100 runs with this parameter setting, 25 resulted in systems with seven vowels. The resulting types of vowel systems are shown in Figure 5.25. There are five types, again identified by letter. Types A and D conform to Crothers's universals 1 to 5, while types B and E conform to his universals 1 to 4, but not to universal 5, which states that languages with seven or more vowels should have either /e o/ or /i ə/. Type C is truly anomalous by conforming only to universals 1 and 5, but not to universals 2 to 4.

The data of Schwartz, Boë, and Vallée (1997) contain 44 systems with seven vowels. Most of these systems, 52 per cent, were of type A. Eighteen per cent were of type E, while 27 per cent were of type D. The remaining vowel system in their data does not fit any type of system that emerged from the simulations. The lack of systems in their data that fit type B is strange, because systems of this type do conform to four of the five 'universals' for vowel systems (just as does type E, which did appear in the data quite frequently). A similar system with *six* vowels, but without the high central vowel (type C for six-vowel systems), does appear in their data. It could be that the low front vowel [a] of type B systems is analysed as a low mid front vowel [ɛ], so that they are classified as type E. The lack of systems of type C for seven-vowel systems is less surprising. This type of system does not conform at all well to Crothers's universals of vowel systems. It contains a low mid central vowel, whereas a mid or high central vowel would be expected. The relatively high frequency of this system can possibly be explained by the fact that the high front vowel seems to be too far to the back in the simulations. Therefore there is less space for a high central vowel, and lower central vowels are preferred, as is the case in four-vowel systems.

5.6.6 *Eight-vowel systems*

Next we consider systems with eight vowels. From the simulation with acoustic noise of 10 per cent, 57 systems with eight vowels emerged. These systems are classified in Figure 5.26. Again, the different types are identified by letter. Types A, B, and C conform to Crothers's universals 1 to 6. Type D does not conform to universal 6, type E does not conform to universal 5, and type F does not conform to universals 3 and 4, but all these

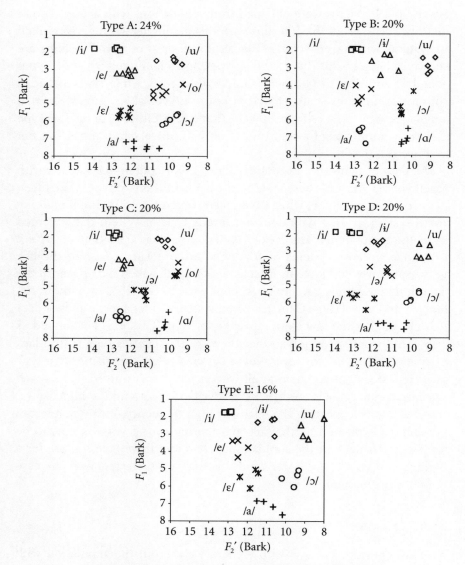

FIGURE 5.25. Classification of seven-vowel systems

types conform to all the other universals. The data of Schwartz, Boë, and Vallée (1997) contained 19 languages with eight vowels, and of these type A occurs in 42 per cent of the cases, type B occurs in 16 per cent, and types C and F in 5 per cent each, that is, one case each. However, another

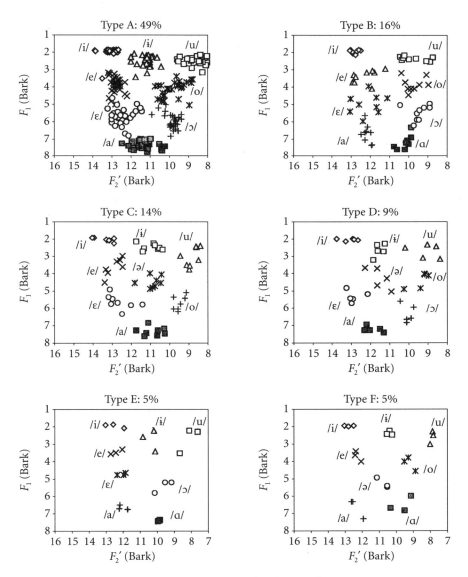

FIGURE 5.26. Classification of eight-vowel systems

four languages in their data seem to have three central vowels. In these systems the central vowels use two levels of height (corresponding to F_1 distinctions) and two levels of position/rounding (corresponding to F_2' distinctions). In the systems that emerged from the simulations, only one degree in the F_2' dimension seems to be used for central vowels. Again this could have to do with the fact that the high front vowel is usually too far to the back in the simulations.

5.6.7 *Nine-vowel systems*

The last group of vowel systems that have been analysed and classified were the nine-vowel systems that emerged from the simulation with $\psi_{ac} = 10$ per cent. Of the 100 vowel systems that emerged, 18 contained nine vowels. Representative agents with these vowel systems are shown in Figure 5.27. In this figure, types A, B, and D conform to Crothers's universals for nine-vowel systems. Type E does not have /o/, so it does not conform to universal 7. It does conform to all other universals, however. Schwartz, Boë, and Vallée (1997) present data on 24 nine-vowel systems. Of these, 29 per cent were of type A, 4 per cent (one system) were of type B, 17 per cent were of either type C or type F, and 4 per cent (one system) were of type D. However, the symmetrical nine-vowel system without central vowels, which accounts for 29 per cent of the cases in their data, does not emerge in our simulations. Nor do systems with three central vowels, just as we found in the case of the eight-vowel system.

5.6.8 *Crothers's others*

There are other universals in Crothers's list that we have not yet checked for in the systems that emerged from the simulations. These are universals 8–12, which are more or less independent of the number of vowels in the vowel system. Universal 8, which states that the preferred number of vowels in a human language is five, cannot be checked with the data that have been used so far. The number of vowels that emerges is dependent on the values of a number of the parameters of the simulation (see the discussion of the parameters earlier in this chapter). Various values were chosen for these parameters in order to obtain interesting and realistic vowel systems with various numbers of vowels. It is therefore impossible to make any comment about the emergence of a preferred number of vowels.

The next section reports an experiment that tries to check the preferred number of vowels in the vowel systems that emerged from the simulations.

Universal 9, which states that the number of height distinctions is equal to or larger than the number of distinctions in the front–back dimension, also appears in the vowel systems that have emerged from the simulations.

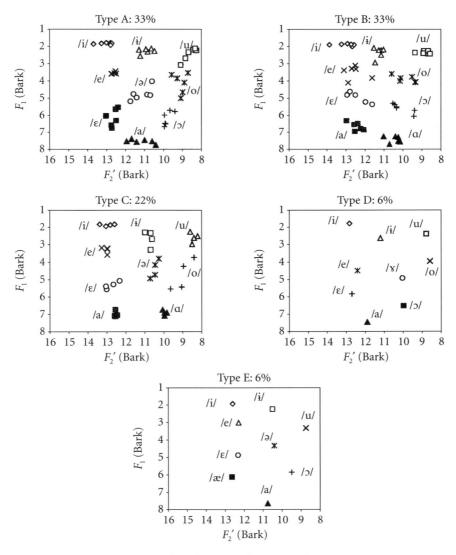

FIGURE 5.27. Classification of nine-vowel systems

None of the emerging vowel systems has more backness distinctions than height distinctions. The systems that emerged also conform to universal 10, which states that systems with two or more interior vowels always have a high one. The only exception to this universal is type F for systems with six vowels (Figure 5.24).

'The number of vowels in a column of interior vowels', states Crothers's (1978) universal 11, 'cannot exceed the number in the front or back columns.' This applies also in the systems that emerged, with the possible exception of type F of the six-vowel systems (Figure 5.24).

Crothers's last universal that is applicable to the systems that emerged from the simulations says that the number of height distinctions in the front column is equal to or greater than the number of height distinctions in the back column. This is not a strong universal, however. Schwartz, Boë, and Vallée (1997) found a number of exceptions. In the systems that emerged there are a number of exceptions to this universal. If we exclude the systems with three vowels (as these will always have an equal number of back and front vowels), 254 vowel systems in total have been classified. Of these vowel systems there were 11 systems (4 per cent) that had more back vowels than front vowels. This finding corresponds well with Crothers's universal 12.

5.6.9 *Preference for a certain number of vowel prototypes*

The last matter that remains to be investigated is whether the sizes of the systems tend towards five vowels. Unfortunately, this does not seem to be the case for the parameter setting used in the experiments presented above. The results of an experiment for investigating whether the systems that emerged have a preference for a certain number of vowels shows (Figure 5.28) that they prefer systems of four vowels. The data in the graph were collected by running the simulation for many different values of the acoustic noise parameter. The standard parameter settings and a population of 20 agents were used. The simulations were run for 25,000 imitation games, as in the other experiments reported in this chapter. The acoustic noise values used were 0.08 to 0.24 with intervals of 0.01 (17 values in total). These values were chosen so that below 0.08 only systems with more than nine vowels occurred, while above 0.24 only systems with fewer than three vowels occurred. Systems with two vowels occur much more frequently, because not all parameter settings for which they emerge have

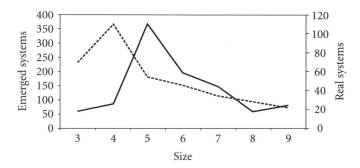

FIGURE 5.28. Distribution of vowel system sizes

Note: The continuous line indicates real systems, the dashed line indicates systems that emerged. Both distributions have a peak that does not fall at the extremes.

been tested. As they occur only very rarely in human systems, however, they have been ignored.

For each of the values of acoustic noise, the simulation was run 100 times. Then the number of times each vowel system size occurred was counted. The number of occurrences of each system size is shown on the left axis and with the dashed line in Figure 5.28. The right axis and the solid line show the size distribution in the data of Schwartz, Boë, and Vallée (1997). The peak at five vowels is very clear.

It can be seen that there is a large preference for systems of four vowels. Both systems of three and five vowels occur less frequently. Although this does not conform to the finding that systems of five vowels occur most frequently in human languages, it does show that the effect of a strong preference for a certain number of vowels also occurs in the systems that emerged. It appears that systems of four vowels are the strongest attractors of the system for the largest range of values of acoustic noise for the specific parameter settings that were used in these experiments.

5.7 Conclusion

The main results of the research described in this book are presented in this chapter. First it was shown that, using the simulation described in the previous chapter, successful and dispersed vowel systems emerge in a population of agents that do not initially have a vowel system. If one changes the parameters of the simulation (for example the acoustic noise level) the shape of the systems that emerge changes, but they remain realistic for a wide range of parameter settings. If one compares the vowel systems that emerged with randomly generated vowel systems on the one hand and with vowel systems that have been optimized for dispersion on the other hand, it is found that the systems that emerged are *much* closer to the optimal vowel systems than to the random ones. Liljencrants and Lindblom (1972) showed that the vowel systems that are most often found in human languages are also often optimally dispersed.

Direct comparison with classifications of human vowel systems has shown that the types of vowel systems that emerge correspond very well with the types of vowel systems that are most often found in human languages. There is even a good correspondence between the frequencies with which different types of vowel systems emerge from the simulation and the frequencies with which these systems actually occur in human languages, at least for vowel systems of between three and nine vowels.

Although the vowel systems were generally presented in acoustic space, and the evaluation of imitation also took place in acoustic space, it has been shown that in articulatory space, too, the systems that emerged show similar tendencies to human vowel systems: front vowels tend to be unrounded, back vowels tend to be rounded, while for low vowels rounding is not well specified.

A further result concerns extending the simulation to changing populations. As human languages persist, even though the individual speakers of the language do not, it was felt to be necessary to investigate whether, in the simulations, vowel systems could persist in changing populations. It was found that vowel systems can indeed persist, if the flux of agents is small enough. If the flux becomes too great, a stable vowel system can still exist, but this will be less complex (that is, have fewer vowels) than in a stable population. It was also shown that a new vowel system can even emerge from scratch in a changing population, although this takes longer than in a stable population. Finally, it was shown experimentally that where agents are restricted to expending a finite amount of effort on learning new vowels, there is an advantage in the fact that old agents can learn less well than young agents.

These results strongly support the hypothesis that self-organization in a population is an important factor in determining the structure of vowel systems. Although the agents neither have innate cognitive predispositions towards vowel systems of a certain structure nor explicitly optimize their vowel system, nevertheless optimal and dispersed vowel systems emerge. They do so as a result of self-organization in a population under constraints of perception and production. And although distinctive features are not necessary in the agent model, it is quite possible to analyse the vowel systems that emerged in terms of distinctive features (see Figure 5.29). The simulations also illustrate that it is possible to test linguistic theories quickly and effectively with computer models.

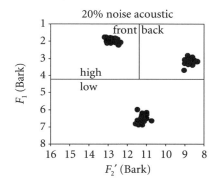 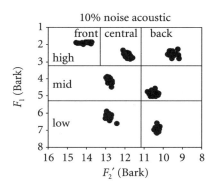

FIGURE 5.29. Distinctive features in emergent vowel systems

Note: Although distinctive features do not figure at all in the way agents produce, perceive, process, and learn vowel systems, they can be used to describe adequately the agents' vowel systems as well as their regularities. The features shown in this figure are not taken from any phonological theory. Rather, they are used to illustrate the fact that the vowel systems can be described in terms of binary and ternary features.

6. Simulated Evolution of Other Parts of Language

In the previous chapters it has been shown that computer simulations can contribute to the understanding of the structure, the emergence, and the evolution of vowel systems. Of course, the evolution of other parts of language can also be investigated by computer simulations and this has been done by a number of researchers in recent years. Research with computer simulations is sometimes referred to as the *modelling* approach to the evolution of language, and has developed in the last ten years or so. Probably the first experiment with a population of communicating agents for linguistic research was described by Hurford (1987, section 6.6). The availability of cheap computing power on the desktop has made it possible to develop the relatively complex simulations that are needed to investigate linguistic phenomena.

This work should not be confused with the older field of computational linguistics. Although there are many similarities between the two fields and although they use the same techniques, their research goals are different: computational linguistics is in general concerned with investigating theories about how language works. The kind of research that will be described in this chapter investigates the origins of language: how can the various structures and phenomena we find in human language have emerged? Usually a part of the simulations is concerned with the adaptive value of the linguistic phenomena under consideration, something with which traditional computational linguistics is not usually concerned.

Most of the computer modelling of language origins has been of syntax and semantics. These are the aspects of language that are generally assumed to be the most typical aspects of human language and thus the most interesting and necessary to explain. Work on the origins of speech sounds was mentioned in Chapter 2. In this chapter, examples of work on syntax, semantics, and language dynamics will be described.

Modelling of language origins is done for two reasons: to learn more about the parts of language modelled and to gain an insight into the dynamics of language as a whole. The research with changing populations of agents described in section 5.4, for example, was intended mainly to investigate language dynamics rather than the properties of vowel systems. A section of this chapter is devoted to research that mainly investigates language dynamics. In practice both goals are often pursued simultaneously.

Some researchers have even attempted to investigate whether robots that have to operate in the 'real' world are able to develop a simple language in order to communicate about objects in their environment or about actions they undertake. The kinds of communication systems these robots develop are more like simple systems of calls than human language, but they are relevant because they directly address the problems of how linguistic signs can be connected to objects and events in the real world. In this respect such experiments are related to experiments with speech sounds. In systems that work with realistic speech sounds it is also necessary to relate an event (a more or less distorted speech signal) to abstract, internal linguistic representations. Therefore some attention will be paid to robotic experiments in this chapter.

The selection of work presented in this chapter is not complete, although I have tried to include references to the work of most important researchers in the field. The criterion of selection has been my own familiarity with the work. To do justice to all the modelling work that has been done on the origins of language would require too much space, even though the field is still very young (see also Hurford *et al.* 1998, Briscoe in press, Studdert-Kennedy *et al.* 2000). The examples have been chosen to provide illustrations of the kinds of work that can be done using computer simulations.

6.1 Modelling of syntax

Syntax has always been considered the most characteristic part of language. It is generally considered to be syntax, or more precisely compositionality, that distinguishes human language from animal communication systems. Because of syntax, human language is not restricted to a possibly large, but finite, number of utterances. It is therefore not surprising that a number of attempts have been made to model the origins of syntax.

However, there are a number of important problems to be overcome when one wants to model syntax. Rules of syntax in human language can often be quite complex, but even simple rules can result in long and complex sentences. In order to model, one has to decide to what level of complexity one wants to model syntax. Does one want to model utterances of fixed length, but in which word order plays a role, or does one want to model utterances in which compositionality plays a role and that are therefore of a length that cannot be fixed beforehand? The modeller also has to decide whether the syntactical rules are innate or whether they are learned, or, as a (realistic) compromise, partly innate and partly learned. Of course, it is also possible to subject the language learners to genetic evolution and see what trade-off between innate and learned knowledge is most adaptive. Finally, in order to do experiments with syntax one has to decide on a simplified model of the semantics that underlie the agents' utterances. Linguistic utterances are not just strings of symbols; their importance is that they have a meaning. The success and adaptiveness of syntactic structures can therefore only be evaluated by how well they are able to convey meanings.

Another important problem with building computer models of syntax is that they involve extraction of patterns and rules from (possibly) inconsistent strings of input data. A full model of the acquisition of language and its syntax would involve learning not only the individual words, but also (possibly guided by innate knowledge) to what category they belong and how they can be combined. This is a much more complicated learning task than the task of coupling individual meanings with individual words that is generally solved in the experiments with meaning (see the next section). Even in the fields of machine learning and computational linguistics the problem of learning syntax has not been completely solved. It is therefore necessary that models of the emergence of syntax make simplifications in the kind of syntax and the kind of utterances that are allowed.

Batali (1998) has investigated models of the emergence of syntax in which agents have to develop a set of sequences of characters that they use to convey simple meanings to each other. The possible meanings are predefined, and the characters that can be used for communication are also predefined, but the mapping between meanings and sequences as well as the actual sequences of characters have to be developed by the agents themselves. The agents use a recurrent neural network for learning the string–meaning couplings. A neural network is a learning mechanism that consists of (computer simulations of) neurons and their interconnections and the inspiration for which is the way the brain works. These models are cognitively plausible, that is, the things they can do can also be done by the human brain. Recurrent neural networks are neural networks in which output or internal neurons are fed back into the input of the network. In this way the network has an internal state (a memory of past events) and can be used to learn sequences.

Batali shows that his agents, starting with a random initialization, can develop a coherent language that can be used successfully for communicating the meanings in the system. The language that emerges has properties that are reminiscent of human language. Sequences can be regularly analysed as consisting of a root and a suffix for most of the expressible meanings, although there are some irregularities. Because of the regularities, his agents are even capable of conveying with some accuracy meanings that they have never used before. In a sense his simple system therefore shows compositionality.

Important research on the modelling of syntax has been done by Kirby (1998, 1999; Kirby and Hurford 1997; see also related work in Hurford 2000). Results of Kirby's research have been published as a book in this series, so I will only discuss his models and results briefly. Kirby uses a population of agents that generate simple, abstract utterances that have some internal structure. These utterances have no explicit meaning, but a predefined parsing complexity can be calculated for each structure. One generation of his agents produces utterances, which can be learned by the next generation, with a probability that depends on their frequency and their parsing complexity. The original agents are removed, and the new generation starts producing utterances, to be learned by the next generation. Although there are generations of agents in his simulation, knowledge is transferred only by learning, not by genetic means. Kirby finds that universal tendencies emerge that are similar to those found in human languages, and that their emergence follows roughly the same dynamics as change in human language. Kirby also investigates different criteria that have to be satisfied in order to prevent the system from rapidly converging to only one possible grammatical structure, something that would contradict the diversity found in human languages. He concludes that locally operating functional pressure gives rise to global universals through cultural mechanisms, rather than through biological mechanisms. He also provides some evidence in support of Universal Grammar, on the basis of certain aspects of language that, according to him, are not adaptive. Finally, he concludes that functional pressure can influence biological evolution, and can therefore give rise to an adaptive innate capacity for language, that is, Universal Grammar.

Steels (1998*b*) has also built a model that can develop a kind of grammar in a population of agents. His agents use much more complicated meanings in order to talk about their environment. The set of possible meanings is open, and consists of semantic trees. These trees are translated into utterances. The model uses symbolic parsing and search mechanisms, rather than neural networks. All words, meanings, and syntactic structures in the system are learned and genetic evolution does not play a role. The utterances do not rely on word order for conveying syntactic relations, but rather on an elaborate system of affixes. No large-scale experiments have yet been done, but experiments with two agents have shown that coherent communication systems can emerge when the agents learn to communicate in this way.

These different simulations have shown that it is possible for populations of agents to develop communication systems that have syntax-like properties. The properties of the communication systems that arise are sometimes reminiscent of the properties of the syntax of human language. Although the kinds of syntax that emerge as well as the underlying semantics are still very simple, it is clear that the modelling approach is able to provide some non-trivial insights about the way in which syntax has developed and about the preconditions that were necessary for syntax to develop.

6.2 Modelling of semantics

In the field of semantics computational models have been built of how agents can develop a way to couple 'meaning' with words (and sometimes combinations of words). In this work different interpretations (or, perhaps more correctly, implementations) of meaning have been used. First, some models contain abstract, autonomous meanings that are generally represented by symbols. In these models, the question of how meanings are related to objects in the world is not addressed. Other models contain objects external to the agents (sometimes called *referents*). Meanings only exist inside the individual agents and might be different for each agent. The meanings are associated on the one hand with a word and on the other hand with a referent. In this latter implementation, it is possible for different meanings (and words) to be associated with the same referent.

A second difference in models of semantics relates to whether there is a fixed set of meanings, or whether the set of meanings is open. In the models where meanings are abstract symbols, there is usually a fixed set, while in the models where meanings are internal to the agent and related to external objects there is usually an open set. Where meanings are abstract and are external to the agents, agents cannot autonomously extend the set of meanings (but the experimenter could, for example, add new meanings to the set).

Finally, meaning as related to an external world can be about objects in the agents' environment (including other agents), about actions that happen in their environment, or even about the results of the actions the agents can undertake themselves (de Jong 1998, 1999). These types of meaning make for challenges of increasing difficulty. Learning meanings for objects is relatively simple and is the most easily understood. Learning meanings for actions is much more difficult as it involves working with classification and recognition of time series. Learning meanings for results of actions that agents undertake is even more difficult as it involves correlating actions with the results of these actions—results that might only be observable some time after the action has finished.

The agents' task in experiments with semantics consists of finding a shared mapping between words and meanings so that successful communication becomes possible. When meanings are internal to the agents, the agents have to find not only the right mapping between words and meanings, but also which meanings to use. When the set of meanings is open and internal to the agents, the agents also have to solve the problem of how and when to add new meanings.

The models usually have a population of agents that interact with each other, comparable to the imitation game described in the previous chapters. In an interaction, it is usual for a topic to be determined first, or generated by the experimenter. Then one agent produces a word and the other agent checks whether this word corresponds to the topic it has. In some models the listening agent then gives feedback about whether the word it heard really corresponds to what it perceives as the topic, but in other models there is no feedback.

Two different ways of changing the associations that the agents have between meanings and words are then possible. The first is comparable to the biological evolution of innate communication systems. In such a system (see, for example, Werner and Dyer 1991) the associations between words and meanings are fixed in an individual. Its performance in interactions determines its fitness, and this fitness determines the likelihood that it is going to create offspring. The offspring will have word–meaning associations that are very similar, but preferably not completely equal, to the ones of the original agent (the offspring might even have new word–meaning associations). In this way a Darwinian evolution of the communication system takes place.

The other way, which is more comparable to the way the imitation games described in this book were implemented, is that the agents actively update the associations they have between words and meanings, as well as their repertoire of words and meanings if necessary. In this way they can learn the word–meaning associations that exist in the population. The two ways may also be combined in a hybrid system. In such a system a part of the word–meaning associations is learned and a part of it is genetically determined.

Many research questions can be addressed by the different simulations. One can investigate, for example, the dynamics in the population, under what circumstances a coherent system is learned, what part of semantics has to be learned and what part has to be genetically determined, or the requirements of a learning system that has to learn the word–meaning associations.

Two researchers (among many, see Steels 1997*b* and Oliphant 1999 for overviews) who have built population-based models of agents acquiring associations between words and meanings are Oliphant (1993, 1996, 1999) and Steels (1995, 1997*b*, 1999). Oliphant was among the first to use population-based models that did not use evolution as the only means of developing, but instead introduced a learning component as well. The aim of Oliphant's research was to investigate under which circumstances 'Saussurean' communication would develop. (Oliphant (1996) states that 'A Saussurean communication system exists when an entire communicating population uses a single language.') He uses a fixed set of symbols and words and his agents' task is to develop associations between words and symbols that are the same for all agents in the population. He shows (Oliphant 1996) that Saussurean communication only emerges if there is a pressure for good transmission. As Oliphant assumes that it is unlikely that there is a direct pressure for good transmission (since it requires effort on the part of the speaker, without providing direct benefit) he shows that it can be achieved either through reciprocal altruism (everybody is both speaker and hearer, so if you want to understand others, it pays to speak intelligibly) or through spatial organization (in which agents that are close together are more likely to interact than those that are far apart). He presents (Oliphant 1999) a system that uses only a very simple learning mechanism that causes a good communication system to emerge. He concludes that the bottleneck for being able to have language cannot be the learning itself, but rather the observation, that is, finding out with which meanings a given signal is to be associated. This problem has also been encountered by researchers trying to implement language learning systems in robots (see below).

Oliphant's work is a good example of simulation work that tries to find out under which circumstances language and communication would evolve and which mechanisms could be responsible for their learning and emergence. Neither the language that is learned nor the learning mechanisms are particularly realistic. Rather the research goal is to find a set of minimal conditions that are necessary for even such a simple system to develop communication. In this respect it is comparable to the research presented in this book. Although realistic models of perception and production were used, the learning mechanism was not particularly realistic. However, it was shown that realistic vowel systems emerged, indicating that self-organization under functional pressure is a phenomenon that can also play a role in shaping language.

Steels's (1995, 1999) work uses an open set of words and meanings. Agents can add new words and new meanings and can therefore create synonymy and homonymy. Also, agents can be added and removed from the population. The agents only learn the language that is spoken; they do not have any innate knowledge, and are also not subject to genetic evolution. His simulations show that a coherent vocabulary can emerge even under these circumstances, lending support to his hypothesis that language is an open, adaptive system (see section 3.1). It was on the basis of these results that it was decided to build the simulations described in this book.

These different interpretations and implementations constitute different simplifications of the problem of how meaning can be coupled to words (or longer utterances). The words used in this kind of work usually do not have an internal structure (although some experiments have been done with multiple word utterances; see, for example, Van Looveren 1999, 2000). However, just as semantic content was ignored in the simulations presented in this book, phonological and phonetic form are ignored in the simulations on semantics. This constitutes another simplification of the problem of coupling meaning with sounds, because in practice the extraction of the linguistic units that correspond with certain meanings is a non-trivial task.

6.3 Modelling of language dynamics

Computer models have not only been used to investigate particular aspects (phonology, syntax, semantics) of language, they have also been used to investigate the dynamics of language. The research on changing populations described in section 5.4 is an example. In such research the aim is not so much to learn more about the particular aspect of language that is modelled in the individual agents, but rather how the language behaves as a phenomenon of the population. Research questions might be how language changes over time, how the spatial distribution of agents influences the development of language, or how the demography of the population of speakers influences the language. In computer models experiments can be done that could never be done with human populations, because in human populations there is no control over the demography and the distribution of the speakers. The influence of these factors can only be investigated by finding different populations in different demographic and spatial situations. However, it is quite possible that two populations in comparable demographic and spatial situations speak languages that are very different. Meaningful comparisons then become very hard. In computer models, linguistic knowledge as well as the demographic and spatial situation can be controlled very precisely. Therefore, the influence of demographic and spatial factors can be investigated precisely.

Traditionally, differences between dialects and historical language change have been described mostly in terms of sound changes and variation of pronunciation. It is therefore not surprising that models of sound change have been among the first models for investigating the dynamics of language (as, for example, described in another book in this series, Nettle 1999). However, other parts of language have been investigated as well, most notably lexicon change and formation (for example, Steels and McIntyre 1999), while Kirby (1999) has used spatial distribution in order to increase variation in his experiments about syntax.

A spatial distribution of the agents in a simulation can be introduced by giving each agent a spatial coordinate, and by defining a function for calculating distances between coordinates. Usually the coordinate will be two-dimensional (inspired by the fact that the surface of the earth is two-dimensional) and the distance function is usually the standard Euclidean distance, corresponding to the way distances are calculated on a plane. Agents will in general be programmed to have a higher probability of communicating with agents that are closer than with agents that are further away. Sometimes there is no real distance function, but rather a neighbourhood function. The agents are imagined as living on a square grid (comparable to a chess board) and agents are only allowed to communicate with their direct neighbours.

Population change can be implemented as described in section 5.4. However, there is another important demographic factor that can be implemented in models of language dynamics, namely, the social status of an agent. In studies of language change (for example, Labov 1994) it has been found that there are certain social groups that tend to lead language changes, while there are other groups that follow. In order to implement social status, agents can be modelled with a social label that other agents can inspect. The probability of agents adapting their linguistic behaviour in the direction of another agent can then be made dependent on their social labels. Even more interesting experiments can be envisaged where agents can know multiple languages (or multiple variants of the same language) at a time and adapt their behaviour to the social situation or even to the language the other agent speaks. As far as I am aware, no experiments have yet been conducted where agents speak multiple languages and are aware of this fact. (However, in Steels 1997c and Steels and McIntyre 1999 a situation emerges where agents speak one language, but are able to understand multiple languages.)

Experiments in modelling language dynamics can be done in different ways. One can start with empty agents and let them develop a language to see what happens when this is done in a population with certain dynamics, instead of a homogeneous population. One can start with agents that are all initialized with the same language and see whether linguistic diversity emerges, or whether all agents will always learn a variant of the same language. Finally one can initialize the agents with carefully prepared different languages and investigate how these influence each other.

An example of work that is concerned primarily with language dynamics, rather than with a particular aspect of language, is the work by Nettle (1999), which has been elaborated upon by Livingstone and Fyfe (1999). The primary aim of this research is to investigate how linguistic diversity can emerge and whether linguistic diversity is inevitable, or something that only emerges under special circumstances. Linguistic diversity is a phenomenon that seems to have its own universal tendencies that are related to social, historical, and geographical factors (see, for example, Nichols 1992, Dixon 1997). Nettle uses a simple simulation of vowel learning in order to investigate the emergence of linguistic diversity in a spatially distributed population of agents. He finds that social selection is necessary in order to have linguistic diversity emerge where there is (even a very low level of) interaction between the spatially distributed groups.

Other work on the dynamics of language has been done by Steels and McIntyre (Steels 1997, Steels and McIntyre 1999). In this research, different populations with different spatial distributions have to learn words for objects in their environment. The agents live on a two-dimensional plane and the distances between them determine the probability that they will interact. It is found that the population learns only one language as long as their distribution is not very clustered. A clustered distribution of agents is a distribution where there are clear groups of agents, each member of which is closer to each of the agents in the same group than to any of the agents in the other groups. If the distribution becomes more clustered,

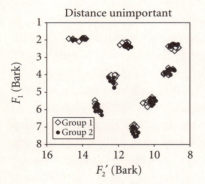 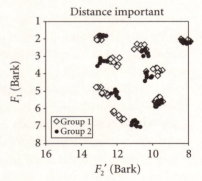

FIGURE 6.1. Results of experiments with spatial distribution

Note: The population of 20 agents is divided into two spatially divided groups of 10. The frame to the left shows what happens when distance does not play a role; after 25,000 games both groups develop the same vowel system. The frame to the right shows what happens if agents have fewer interactions if they are further apart. Both groups develop vowel systems that are different but related (there are still some interactions). The systems could be considered dialectal variants.

different languages will emerge. However, because there are still interactions between clusters (although they are rarer), the above-mentioned multilingual situation will emerge: agents will be able to understand the words produced by agents from another cluster, but they will only be able to produce words from the language in their own cluster. An example of vowel imitation games in which the population was divided into two spatially distributed groups is given in Figure 6.1.

Although the underlying linguistic models might be simplistic, the simulations of language dynamics can provide valuable insights into the dynamics of human language. There are different theories of how languages change over time and how they are influenced by demographic and spatial factors. All these theories are based on the same observations, and it is sometimes very hard to tell which theories are right, because experimental testing in human populations is impossible, for obvious reasons. Computer implementations, however, can test the dynamics predicted by the different theories. A theory that predicts the dynamics that are most easily reproduced by computer models is more likely to be right than other theories. Further empirical sociolinguistic observations can then be collected in order to refine both theories and models.

6.4 Experiments with robots

An interesting extension of the use of computer models to investigate language is the transfer of the computer models to experiments with robots. Such experiments are quite a long way from mainstream linguistics. Many linguists tend to be somewhat sceptical about the use of computer models for investigating language, so it is to be expected that experiments with robots, which are already more controversial in artificial intelligence research (the field where such experiments originated), will encounter even more scepsis. Nevertheless, experiments that use robots are just a logical extension of experiments with computer simulations. Such experiments with robots are interesting and they can contribute to our understanding of the problems encountered in learning a language and of the possible solutions to these problems.

The robots that are used in the experiments are not at all like the industrial robots that are used in the manufacturing of, for example, cars, nor are they like the humanoid robots seen in science fiction films. More usually they are small, wheeled vehicles that are equipped with a number of simple sensors. Such sensors usually include touch sensors that are used for detecting if the robot has collided with an object or a wall, infrared sensors for detecting obstacles from a distance, and different light sensors for detecting and identifying different objects in their environment. (Two such robots are shown in Figure 6.2.) For modelling linguistic communication, the robots often have small digital radios. The more sophisticated robots have small television cameras with which they can perceive their environment visually. In fact these robots are quite comparable to the robots that are used in the RoboCup robot soccer competition (Kitano *et al.* 1997). In addition to being used for experiments with language, such robots have been used to investigate among other things learning behaviour, foraging behaviour, and co-operation.

The environments in which the robots operate are usually small, confined spaces containing a number of objects, obstacles, or other robots. Although not as complex as, and more controlled than, the real world, these environments are much more complex and real than anything that can be modelled in simulations. Whereas in simulations variation is introduced by adding random noise from some kind of constant distribution, in experiments with real robots, variation is more often caused by systematic errors, such as unexpected sensor properties, changes in position of objects in

FIGURE 6.2. Two of Vogt's robots playing a 'follow me' game
Note: The robot on the right is following the white light source on the robot on the left.

the environment, changes in lighting conditions, and changes in battery level. As no statistical assumptions can be made about such errors, they are impossible to filter out by statistical techniques, and the robots have to adapt to them or at least be sufficiently robust to be able to continue to work despite them.

The challenges encountered by a robot operating in even a reasonably controlled environment are therefore much more like the challenges encountered by an infant learning language than those encountered by agents in a computer simulation. Another aspect of robotic experiments is that there is a limit to the number of times a robot can repeat an action before learning it, as well as a limit to the amount of time available to do this. In computer simulations it is often possible to iterate a learning algorithm thousands of times in a matter of seconds (and the vowel imitation games described in this book are no exception), but in reality learning must often proceed much more efficiently. For this reason, too, experiments on real robots are interesting, because they force the experimenter to try only the models that work in a reasonable amount of time.

Because of the lack of time and the imprecision of observations, robots cannot model their environment completely. Classical control algorithms that first model the environment, then reason about the environment, and finally plan an action have therefore been found to be unsatisfactory (Brooks 1990, 1991). Usually the robots are equipped with a control architecture that consists of a layer that implements basic survival strategies (such as avoidance of obstacles and collision detection) in a *reactive* way. Reactive behaviour is behaviour in which sensory inputs are directly translated into actions. Such behaviour can be compared with reflexive behaviour in humans. If, for example, we touch a hot object, we retract our hand automatically, without conscious action.

However, purely reactive behaviour is by definition insufficient for language. Therefore the robots that are used in investigating language are equipped with a second layer that implements the robot's linguistic behaviour. The reactive layer has priority over the language layer. When the robot hits a wall while talking to another robot, for example, it will first try to free itself from the wall, even though this might disrupt the conversation with the other robot. In this respect such behaviour is comparable to human behaviour, where reflexes also have priority over 'higher' behaviour.

The importance of experiments with robots is that they need to solve a number of problems whose solution is usually taken for granted because humans are so good at solving them. One such problem is how patterns of sounds, which are subject to complicated variations and combinations with other sounds, come to be associated with objects in the environment that do not give a constant sensory impression either. How is an association learned, even though the sounds and the objects might be different each time they are observed and may co-occur with other sounds and objects? The problem of perceiving an object as constant even though the exact sensory impressions change is known as the object constancy problem. A real robot has to solve this problem at least partly, in order to be able to learn words for objects. Another problem is how robots can attract each other's attention to a desired object in their environment. Choosing a topic of conversation is usually taken for granted in computer simulations (although see Steels and Kaplan 1997), but it turns out to be a serious problem with real robots. Yet another problem is how words for actions (verbs) can be learned. Actions take place over a period of time and do not always have a clear beginning or end. Also, because of their duration actions are harder to classify and distinguish than objects. Learning words for them is therefore even harder than learning words for objects.

There is a parallel between the problems faced by experiments with real robots and problems faced by a computer model that tries to learn and use realistic complex utterances. Such utterances consist of a string of basic sounds that influence each other and that might sound slightly different every time they are pronounced, especially if they are pronounced by different speakers. This raises an object constancy problem similar to the one faced by robots talking about objects in their environment. Another parallel occurs because complex utterances extend over time, and the individual phonemes or syllables that make up the utterance do not have a clear beginning or end in time, as is true of the actions of real robots. There are fewer such parallels between simplified computer simulations and imitation games with complex utterances. It is therefore likely that the algorithms that can be used to solve the question of how real robots learn meanings can also help to extend the learning and imitation of complex speech sounds.

Examples of work on robots that learn and develop language include the work by Vogt (Steels and Vogt 1997, Vogt 2000) and that of Billard and Hayes (1998, 1999), as well as Steels's talking heads experiment (Steels 1998*b*). In Vogt's as well as in Billard and Hayes's research projects, mobile robots learn to communicate about objects in their environment and actions they can undertake. In Steels's experiment two movable cameras learn a vocabulary and a set of associated meanings about two-dimensional geometrical objects on a blackboard. Steels's experiments are more controlled and hence closer to a simulation than either of the other projects. Vogt's experiments are concerned with naming and discriminating between objects in the environment and with naming and discriminating between actions that are observed being performed by another robot. In the object-naming task, two robots ride around in a simple environment in which different objects can be distinguished by their properties in the visible light and infrared spectrum. Every once in a while, one of the two robots chooses an object as a topic of conversation, indicates this to the other robot, and produces a word. The other robot checks whether this word corresponds to what it thinks the topic of conversation is, and learns it if necessary. A robot may also learn new sensory distinctions that are necessary for discriminating between different objects. After a while, a relatively successful lexicon of shared words emerges. But not only do the agents develop a shared set of words, they also develop a similar set of sensory distinctions (that is, a way of looking at the world), although they cannot directly observe each other's sensory distinctions. In Vogt (2000) this system is extended to discriminating between and naming actions performed by the robots, inspired by Billard and Hayes's (1999) work. In both projects, two robots follow each other. In order to follow, the following robot is forced to imitate the other robot's actions. The leading robot names the actions it undertakes. If the following robot is able to match the words to actions, it will be able to follow the first robot better.

The main difference between Vogt's and Billard and Hayes's work, at least from the perspective of linguistics, is that in Vogt's experiments, both robots contribute to the formation of the lexicon, and the number of words is in principle unlimited. In Billard and Hayes's experiments, one agent is assigned the role of teacher and one is assigned the role of student, with the teacher's lexicon being predefined. Not surprisingly, Billard and Hayes's robots learn slightly more quickly and more effectively than Vogt's robots. Also, Billard and Hayes's architecture is more general than Vogt's architecture. However, both experiments show that it is possible, using relatively simple means, to form and learn a lexicon of words and that this can happen quickly and reliably.

Of course, these experiments cover only a very small part of the problems of language learning and language origins. The robots that are used are extremely simple in comparison with humans, and so are the 'languages' they learn. But ultimately applicability in the real world is the test that any theory about language should pass.

6.5 Relation to the work described here

Although the work described above is extremely diverse and investigates the modelling of (the origins of) language in many different ways and from many different theoretical perspectives, it is all relevant to the work on phonology described in this book. First of all, many of the experiments shed light on the question whether self-organization could play a role in other parts of language as well. As will be elaborated in the next chapter, the results obtained so far indicate that this is indeed the case.

Also, the attempts at modelling different aspects of language show the strengths and weaknesses of the methodology of building computer models. Computer models provide a powerful means of investigating how a theory that is concerned with the dynamics of language behaves. Complex dynamic systems such as a population of communicating agents can sometimes show surprising behaviour that would be impossible to predict without simulation. Examples of such surprising behaviour include the emergence of the human-like vowel systems and a preference for a certain size of vowel system in the simulations described in this book, or the emergence of affixes in Batali's (1998) simulations. Therefore computer models can provide extra support for theories about language. However, as in every computer simulation, simplifications have to be made, and as these simplifications influence the outcome of the simulation, computer modelling alone can never give us all the answers. An interaction is necessary between the computer models and the knowledge we have about natural language and human language behaviour (learning, use, speech errors, aphasia, etc.). Therefore, I argue that computer models should stay as close as possible to actual human linguistic behaviour, as this makes comparing the result with natural languages easier and less prone to errors of interpretation, or a tendency to see linguistically relevant results in phenomena that are just the expected behaviour of any dynamic system. In this respect, experiments with phonology and phonetics should be less controversial than experiments with syntax or semantics, as phonology and phonetics are the parts of language that are most objectively measurable. Phonetics and phonology are therefore the fields of choice if one wants to investigate the dynamics of language (as investigated by Nettle (1999) and Livingstone and Fyfe (1999)).

Another benefit of making computer models is that they force researchers to make their assumptions explicit. For example, it is easy to assume in a theory that it is possible to pick a topic of conversation that is unambiguous, but experiments with robots have shown that this is not an easy task. The ability to know what the topic of conversation is should therefore be present before language can develop, both in an individual and in a species. However, other experiments have shown that a certain degree of uncertainty in determining the topic is not a problem for learning a communication system (Steels and Kaplan 1997). The general outcome of building computer models of language (and indeed a general outcome of all artificial intelligence research) is that many of the basic faculties that are taken for granted in humans are not so simple after all. This is not necessarily a problem for theories on the origins of language, it just indicates that early hominids (as well as apes, probably) must have had very sophisticated cognitive skills.

A final relation between the work described in this chapter and the work on phonology is that in human language, no part of language operates completely autonomously. As Steels (1997b) observed, different parts of language exert pressure on each other. A large lexicon makes it necessary to make accurate phonological distinctions, but the fact that a lexicon is finite makes it necessary for syntax to exist. Phonological changes exert pressure on the lexicon when differences between words disappear, while they also cause changes of the grammar when affixes are reduced. Also, the lexicon can exert pressure on the grammar when independent words become grammaticalized into grammatical words or affixes. Therefore, modelling any part of language in isolation is in fact a very large simplification. Whenever one wants to build a model of the whole of language, all aspects of language have to be taken into account. The building of such a model is of course still far in the future. Nevertheless, all the separate modelling efforts contribute to this final goal.

7.   Implications for Other Parts of Language

The main contribution of the work described in this book has been to show that vowel systems with the same universal tendencies as human vowel systems can emerge as the result of self-organization in a population of agents. The agents do not have an innate disposition towards learning and using certain vowel systems, nor do they explicitly optimize their vowel systems. Rather, the universal tendencies seem to be an unavoidable outcome of the articulatory and perceptual constraints of the agents as well as their participation in numerous repeated interactions in which they have only limited information and in which errors can occur. Even if the parameters of the system, or the rules of the game, are slightly changed (for more details see de Boer 1999), the same kinds of vowel systems emerge.

7.1 Interpretation of results

From a dynamic systems perspective these results can be explained as follows. The perception, production, and learning of the individual agents, together with their interactions, form a complex dynamic system. This system shows self-organization in the sense described in Chapter 3. In such a system there are attractors, that is, a limited (but usually not extremely small) number of states to which the system will tend to evolve over time. The dynamics of the system cause certain configurations of vowels to be stronger attractors than others. An attractor is stronger if there are more initial states from which the system will evolve towards it. Therefore, starting from an initial random configuration, the system will tend to evolve most often towards the strongest attractors.

It should be noted that because of random variations in the dynamic system (on production of the vowels, on the way agents and vowel prototypes are chosen, and on the insertion of new vowel prototypes), the vowel systems will not generally settle in an attractor, but will keep on changing. Therefore, the term 'attractor' cannot be used in its mathematical sense, but is used here in a looser sense as a set of states towards which the system evolves. In linguistic terms, these states correspond to vowel systems that are phonologically identical, but in which individual realizations of vowels differ somewhat and might change over time. The vowel systems evolve towards these final states if they are far away and move around them if they are nearby. However, it should be kept in mind that if random fluctuations accumulate the system can move towards a different attractor (in linguistic terms a system that would be different phonologically).

Because the system is so complex, there are many attractors. For this reason, the vowel systems that are found are not always the ones in which the dispersion of the vowel prototypes is maximal (which would be only one configuration for every given number of vowels). Non-optimal systems appear because the evolution of the vowel systems is determined by their successfulness in imitation. The success in imitation of an agent's vowel prototypes is not just determined by their distribution through acoustic space, but also by the extent to which they resemble the vowel prototypes of the other agents in the population. There is no advantage to be gained from optimizing an individual vowel system if doing so makes it impossible to imitate the other agents in the population. It is therefore possible for vowel systems to emerge that are sub-optimal in terms of acoustical distinctiveness or articulatory ease, but that are nevertheless retained because they are shared by the majority of agents in the population. An individual agent might be able to move its vowels to make its vowel system more optimal, but this would reduce its success in imitation since the other agents still stick to the old system. Therefore, once the system reaches a sub-optimal state it will tend to stay there.

In their study on predicting vowel systems, Liljencrants and Lindblom (1972) noted that the success of individual vowels does not depend on their absolute position in acoustic space, but on their position relative to the other vowels in the system. The present study has shown that there is the added requirement to conform to the population. Success also depends on the positions of the vowels of the other members of the population.

However, it is impossible for an attracting vowel system to be entirely bad for imitation purposes. It would not be stable enough, and the slightest random variation would move the system away from it and towards a more optimal attractor. This reflects the situation in human languages: not all vowel systems found in human languages are optimal, but none of the systems is very bad from either an articulatory or a perceptual point of view.

7.2 Implications for universals of vowel systems

We now turn to the question of the implications of the results of this modelling study for the study of the universals of human vowel systems. After all, the results are based on a simplified model of what happens in human language. In the model there are only vowels produced in isolation, while in human languages there are all kinds of other sounds, produced in combinations that influence each other. In the model there is no meaning, but only a very crude and unrealistic feedback signal about whether an imitation was successful or not. Finally, the way the agents in the simulation learn is probably quite unlike the way in which children learn. However, I would argue that the aspects that are crucial for understanding the universal tendencies of vowel systems are captured in the simulation. It has been shown in previous work (for example Liljencrants and Lindblom 1972, Carré 1996) that universal properties of (small) vowel systems can be predicted from simple acoustic and articulatory properties of vowels in isolation. Also, the articulatory model and the perceptual model are sufficiently realistic, while at the same time being sufficiently general and not limited to the sounds of particular languages. The use of computer models of populations of agents in order to study properties of language has already been shown to give interesting and relevant results in other areas (see Chapter 6 and sections 2.8 and 2.9). The argument that computer models only produce what one has put in at the start is not valid when one studies the phenomena that emerge in complex dynamic systems. Such systems are too complex for their behaviour to be predicted from their basic dynamics. The only way to know their behaviour is to simulate them.

What was tested here was the hypothesis that self-organization occurs in a population of agents that interact using speech sounds and that it is responsible for the universals that are observed. The hypothesis has been confirmed by the experiments. The implication for the study of human vowel systems is therefore that self-organization in the population should be taken into account as a mechanism for explaining universals.

Universals are now no longer to be considered the result of purely individual factors, such as innate disposition towards certain structures, possibly driven by a Universal Grammar, or an individual tendency towards optimization of communicative success. The role of the communication system in the population and the interactions between agents also have to be taken into account.

This makes it necessary to view the sound system as a dynamic, social phenomenon as well as viewing it as an abstract capacity of an individual. In order to understand a sound system, its history is as important as the capacities and knowledge of the individual speakers. Such a point of view may help to bridge the (apparently rather artificial) distinction between diachronic and synchronic linguistics.

7.3 Self-organization and other aspects of language

It is tempting to speculate a little about the meaning for other parts of linguistics of the findings reported in this book. Of course, the results in this book relate only to vowel systems, so there is no substantial proof that self-organization also plays a role in other parts of language, or even in sounds that are more complicated than simple vowels. However, there are good reasons to expect self-organization to play a role in other parts of language as well. First of all, self-organization is a phenomenon that occurs in many different complex natural systems, so it is reasonable to expect a priori that it also plays a role in language. Furthermore, related research has shown that in the realm of lexicon formation and innovation (Steels 1995), the formation and sharing of semantic distinctions (Steels 1997*a*, Steels and Vogt 1997), and the formation of syntax (Batali 1998, Steels 1998*a*, Kirby and Hurford 1997, Kirby 1998, Kirby 1999, Hurford 2000) the mechanisms of self-organization and cultural evolution also play an important role. However, these models were more abstract and therefore their results are more difficult to compare and verify with real linguistic data. This section and the next two sections explore in a more speculative way the possible relevance of the work described here for other aspects of language.

In the research into vowel systems described in this book, the universal tendencies of human vowel systems were used as a means of testing the predictions made by the computational model. Using the properties of a single language to build or test a hypothesis in this framework is not possible. As was made clear, the history of a self-organizing system depends in part on its dynamics and in part on random factors (its initial state and random[1] influences on its history). Therefore a single language might have

---

[1] Of course, neither 'random' influences (nor the initial state, if it is at all meaningful to speak about an initial state in the case of language) are ever really random. What is meant is that they cannot be modelled properly.

idiosyncratic properties. For example, it would not be a good idea to base a theory of the properties of vowel systems on the vowel system of English alone. The vowel system of English is exceptionally large, and does not conform very well to Crothers's (1978) universals. A similar methodology would have to be followed for other parts of language. Any predictions of a theory that involves self-organization should be compared with the universals of human language.

Inherent in a theory that involves self-organization is that language changes over time. This means that language is variable, that individuals must be able to produce different variants of utterances, and that different individuals might use different versions of the language. In this framework, sociolinguistic variation as well as historical change have to be considered integral aspects of a synchronic description of the language. In a model of vowels it is still quite easy to imagine how this works: variation within individuals is modelled as addition of random noise, while variation between individuals can be modelled as slightly different vowel prototypes. It is harder to imagine how this works in more 'discrete' parts of language, such as syntax. Nevertheless it is essential for a theory of self-organization to identify the possible ways in which the aspect of language to be modelled can vary within and between individuals.

Also, for a theory of self-organization in language it is necessary to identify the functional pressures on the system. It is necessary to know how difficult it is to use and learn different variations of the modelled part of language. This determines the dynamics of the system and therefore where its attractors are. Preferably the pressures on the system should be derived from language-independent considerations. These could be physical or communication theoretical, but also psycho-acoustical or cognitive. Pressures that are derived from observations of language itself should be avoided, as they carry the risk of rendering the theory circular, in that it needs the phenomena to be explained as a precondition for the model that is used as an explanation.

Finally, an explanation of linguistic phenomena (whether involving self-organization or not) should not just be a purely philosophical and speculative discourse. The theory should make testable predictions. The predictions can either be of a broad nature, such as, in the example of the vowel system, that dispersed vowel systems are preferred, or be of a narrower kind, for example that systems with more front vowels are preferred to systems with more back vowels. Predictions of models with self-organization can be made in two ways: by analysis of the proposed process, and by computer simulations. The analysis method will generally result in broad predictions, while the computer simulations will result in narrower predictions. However, the analysis can suggest computer simulations, and computer simulations can aid the analysis of the complex dynamics of the system.

Let us now consider a number of examples of how self-organization could play a role in other parts of language, how variation could occur, and what universals could be considered for testing the model. These examples should be considered as illustrations of how theories about self-organization could be constructed and not be taken too seriously as linguistic theories. Although I hope that the ideas presented here can contribute a little to the explanation of the phenomena under study, I really do not know enough about the different linguistic subjects to defend the theories confidently.

The first example concerns syntax. An interesting observation about the syntax of human languages is that certain word orders seem to be preferred to others. In a simple transitive sentence there are three constituents: the subject, the object, and the verb. These constituents are usually symbolized with the letters S, O, and V, respectively. Many languages tend to prefer a fixed order for these constituents. English, for example, prefers the word order SVO, as in the sentence 'Mary kisses John'. There are languages that do not have a strong preference for word order, such as classical Latin, Russian, and the Australian aboriginal language Dyirbal (Dixon 1972), but these can be considered irrelevant for study of word order universals. With the three constituents there are six possible sequences: SOV, SVO, VSO, VOS, OVS, and OSV. It has been found by comparing many different languages (Greenberg 1966, referenced in Comrie 1981, ch. 4) that certain word orders occur more frequently than others. Word orders where the subject precedes the object are relatively frequent, while word orders where the object precedes the subject are much rarer. One may of course assume that humans are innately predisposed towards a certain ordering of constituents, but then one would have to find an evolutionary explanation of how this has become so, or how this could be a side effect of other properties of the human brain. Also, although they are rare and have a limited geographical distribution (especially object-initial languages: see Derbyshire and Pullum 1981), languages with all possible word orders do exist. It would be easier to accept an innate constraint if there were no exceptions. However, the debate is still open, but the challenge here is to propose an explanation based on independent factors and the dynamics of a population of language users and learners. In fact Kirby's (1999) work was partly on word order but involved more than only subject, object, and verb. He showed how preferences for certain word orders could emerge through use in a population as well as how such preferences could become innate, or be influenced by pre-existing innate tendencies.

The first question to ask is: what are the functional pressures on agents that try to communicate with simple transitive sentences? Agents have to encode and decode the roles of the different actors in the sentence. Languages have found several possibilities for doing this. One possibility is obviously word order. If word order is fixed, roles can be unambiguously assigned. However, another possibility is to use morphology. The words in the sentence for the different actors can be given affixes that indicate their roles and these roles might also be indicated on the verb. In this case a fixed word order is not necessary. I will make no assumptions about the complexity of parsing sentences with morphology or sentences with different word orders, as very little is known about exactly how humans parse sentences. Nor will I make assumptions about whether it is more difficult to learn a mapping between morphology and syntactic roles or between word order and syntactic roles. However, an assumption that can be made is that morphology tends to erode over time. This has been attested in the history of many languages.

Another assumption that can be made is about the nature of the syntactic subject. According to Comrie (1981) subjects are difficult to define exactly. However, whenever the verb of the sentence is conjugated, it tends to accord with the subject, and subjects are prototypically the agent and the topic of a sentence. The agent is the entity performing the action, while the topic of a sentence is usually whatever the conversation (in which the sentence is uttered) is about. It is entirely possible to construct a sentence in which the subject is neither the agent nor the topic, but generally the syntactic role of subject, the pragmatic role of topic, and the semantic role of agent tend to coincide. This is to be expected on communication theoretical grounds and the way in which conversations are usually structured. In a conversation, different consecutive sentences will generally be about the same agent, so that topic and agent coincide. Also, an action is often most closely associated with the agent performing it, so it seems logical that a verb would more often be inflected according to the agent of the sentence than according to other actors.

Another observation about the way sentences are formed is that the topic of a sentence is often placed at the beginning. This is also understandable from a communication theoretical point of view. It is easier to interpret a sentence if one already knows the topic of the sentence. Psycholinguistic experiments have shown that lexical access is faster when subjects already have a clue about what the word they hear might mean. This is called semantic priming.

We have thus a situation in which language users have a tendency to associate subject, agent, and topic of a sentence and to place topics at the beginning of the sentence. This opens up the possibility for there to be a directed positive feedback loop in a population. Suppose we start with a language where all word orders are allowed, and which therefore must have morphological means (or a means based on grammatical function words) to indicate the different roles. However, sentences in which the subject is first will occur slightly more often, because subject tends to be associated with topic and topic will tend to be put first in a sentence. New language learners will observe this and learn a slight preference for subject-first sentences. This process can become a positive feedback loop, especially if the morphological clues tend to get lost through phonetic erosion of the affixes. Hence the preference for subject before object cross-linguistically.

Of course, the question remains why there are still languages in which the object comes before the subject. It is quite possible that the preference for putting the subject first in languages where word order is free is very small, and that historically morphemes might disappear very quickly, so that a given word order is petrified before the positive feedback loop can have much effect. Other aspects of the language might also play a role in favouring different word orders, such as the order of other constituents of the sentence, for example adjectives and nouns, or whether the language uses prefixes or suffixes.

A broad prediction of a model of self-organization in word order would be that object-first languages are much rarer than subject-first languages. However, this is likely to be incorporated in the simulation, as this was known beforehand. Less broad predictions might concern the position of the verb in the sentence as, among object-first languages for example, VOS languages are much more common than OSV languages. Ideally, a model should generate the word orders in about the same ratios as those in which they occur in natural languages. Other predictions might concern the dynamics of the process. From the argument in the previous paragraph it could be predicted that object-first languages will tend to appear in situations where change of the mechanism that determines the syntactic roles (morphology, grammatical function words, or a different word order) happens relatively quickly. In such a situation the feedback loop that causes the preference for subject-first word order does not have much time in which to operate.

The second example of the possible role of self-organization concerns tones in language and how they can arise. A tone language is a language in which the pitch, or the pitch contour with which a syllable is pronounced, can change the meaning of the word containing it (see, for example, Laver 1994, ch. 15, for an overview). The best-known tone language is (Mandarin) Chinese, which has four tones, but tone is a phenomenon that occurs in many different languages all over the world. Although less is known about universals of tone than about universals of vowel systems, there still seem to be a number of universal tendencies of tone systems. These have to do with their size, the different combinations of tones, and the way tones interact with the phonemes of the language (see, for example, Maddieson 1978).

Historically, tone languages develop out of languages that do not have tone. This is slightly puzzling, as it might seem that a language either has tones or does not have tones. Therefore one could imagine that there must be a moment where the language undergoes a sudden transition from having no tones to having tones. This seems to conflict with the gradualness of language change, which proceeds almost imperceptibly to the speakers of the language.

However, it must be kept in mind that tone is a *phonological* phenomenon. The emergence of tone in a language usually occurs because of loss of a conditioning environment that determines the (phonetic) intonation of words. Consonants tend to alter the pitch of the vowels that occur around them. In the history of a language it can happen that the consonants are lost, but the intonation contours are preserved (for an overview of possible mechanisms see, for example, Hock 1991, section 5.4 and references therein). Some syllables might then appear that were formerly distinguished by their consonants, but that are now distinguished only by their pitch contour. In this way, tone has become a mechanism with which the meaning of a word can be changed, and has therefore become phonological.

The crucial point here is that the intonation contours already exist before the consonants are lost. If one considers language as a changeable-population phenomenon, one can imagine a population in which the speakers have different variants of the language. In some, more informal, variants the consonants are not pronounced, because of the functional pressure of ease of pronunciation. But as the speakers do know the more complete variants, they produce the intonation contours as if the consonants were still there. In this stage speakers might even claim that they produce a consonant, even if from an articulatory point of view this is not the case. The functional pressure of avoiding too many similar words with different meanings forces the speakers to retain this contour. Children who learn the language at this stage might learn a preference for the words in which the consonants have been swallowed, and the language might change to a tone language. In this way, the language changes from not having tones to having tones without any abrupt transitions.

Strictly speaking there is no self-organization in this process, except perhaps in causing the language to stay coherent (all speakers lose the same consonants and replace them with the same tones) even though it changes. However, it does involve the concepts of language variation within and between individuals, as well as functional pressure and the transfer of language from one generation to the next. Therefore self-organization could occur and it would be worthwhile to check whether universals of tone could be explained as the result of self-organization. At the moment, however, it is still impossible to build a realistic model of the emergence of tones.

The last example I will give concerns a universal tendency of consonant systems (already mentioned in section 2.1), which is that they tend to be symmetrical with respect to voiced and voiceless plosives. Whenever a language has a voiced plosive at a given point of articulation (for example a /d/) it tends to have a voiceless plosive at the same place of articulation (in the example a /t/) as well. This symmetry might be explained as the result of a tendency towards the reuse of the feature 'voiced' at different places of articulation, but from the point of view of self-organization, another explanation can be given.

Suppose a language does not make the (phonological) distinction between voiced and voiceless plosives. Suppose such a language has an alveolar plosive, which will be written as /T/. It can be realized as either [t] or [d], but this will not make a distinction in meaning. If there is a word /aT/ it can be pronounced either [at] or [ad]. This phenomenon is called free variation between voiced and voiceless variants. Usually, in careful speech one of the two is preferred. However, in fast, informal speech articulatory ease causes the plosives to become voiced if they occur between other voiced segments (vowels, for example). A hypothetical word /aTa/ would tend to be pronounced [ada]. Whenever they occur at the edge of a word (especially at the end) they will tend to become voiceless, so that the hypothetical word /aT/ would be pronounced [at]. It is likely that this pronunciation will become the standard pronunciation after a while, as children would be exposed to the informal variant more often than to the formal variant. Now another variant of the language might appear in which certain syllables at the edge of the word are no longer pronounced. This is also a phenomenon that is observed in fast, informal speech. But these might be the syllables that formerly conditioned the plosives to become voiced. A minimal pair between a voiced and a voiceless plosive might now arise if there is a monosyllabic word that has the same beginning as the word that is being reduced. However, in the monosyllabic word the plosive is produced voiceless and in the reduced word the plosive is produced voiced. Language users might retain the distinction in pronunciation under the functional pressure of avoidance of homonymy. In our example the word /aTa/ will get the reduced pronunciation [ad], which will now form a minimal pair with the word /aT/, pronounced [at]. The phoneme /T/ is now split into a phoneme /t/ and a phoneme /d/.

This is an example of how a language can change from having no phonological distinction between voiced and unvoiced stops to having such a distinction. The steps in this process are all based on modifications of pronunciation that occur in fast speech, and that are therefore likely to occur. There are undoubtedly processes by which the distinction between voiced and unvoiced stops is lost, but these might be less likely. The transition from a language without a voiced/voiceless distinction to a language that does make the distinction is therefore more likely than vice versa. This explains why languages that have symmetrical consonant systems with respect to voicing are more common than languages that do not.

Again, as in the case of the formation of tones, the explanation is based on functional pressures of ease of pronunciation and homonymy avoidance and can take place because there is linguistic variation within and between individuals. The system self-organizes towards symmetrical consonant systems.

These examples illustrate that other aspects of language can also be investigated from the point of view of self-organization. Of course, the examples given here are purely speculative, and it might well be that the arguments contain serious flaws. However, they are mostly meant to illustrate the way an investigation that takes the dynamics of a population into account could proceed. Traditionally universals have been explained as due to (innate, cognitive, or functional) properties of the language users or historical accidents or because all languages are historically related. The study of language from the point of view of self-organization opens up the possibility of a fourth factor. Universals might be the result of population dynamics in combination with properties of individuals. Such explanations would be more satisfying than those based on historical accident or deep historical relations between languages, and easier from an evolutionary point of view than explanations based on innate properties of individuals.

7.4 Implications for more complex sounds

So far all the results presented in this book have been about vowels. Are these results in any way relevant for more complex utterances? And what would be the importance of a self-organizing model of such utterances? Human speech does not consist of vowels pronounced in isolation. Rather it consists of sequences of complex, highly co-ordinated utterances in which many different articulatory actions take place that can influence each other through co-articulation. Systems of human speech sounds contain many different consonants of different articulatory complexity and show a whole range of universal tendencies. Human speech consists of syllables that make up words, and there are very many partly learned, partly physical rules that determine how speech sounds in sequence influence each other. The form of syllables also shows a great many different universals (see section 2.2). Not all of these universals have yet been explained.

The relevance of the results obtained so far for the study of more complex sounds is mainly that they illustrate that computer models of self-organization in sound systems are able to provide interesting insights into universals. As was pointed out in the previous section, it is quite possible that a number of universals of more complex utterances can also be explained as the result of self-organization in a population. A model of a population of agents that learn and use a system of more complex sounds would help to substantiate or refute these ideas.

Models of more complex utterances are interesting not only for providing insights into universals of systems of such utterances; they are also necessary for the conduct of investigations into universals of language change. Although the vowel systems that emerged in the simulations described in this book were not quite static, and could change over time, the way in which they changed was not completely realistic. What happens in reality is that systems of speech sounds sometimes undergo changes as a whole. An example would be a chain shift in which all vowels change position as if they were pushing or pulling each other along. Another change of a vowel system as a whole is the appearance or disappearance of modified vowels, such as nasalized or long ones. Such modified vowels often appear or disappear as a group. For other speech sounds, such as consonants and syllables, there are also universals of language change.

Sound change is often caused because speech sounds appear in context. Co-articulation tends to modify sounds in certain positions, and these changes might become permanent, especially when the modifying context is lost, as was seen above in the examples of tones and of voicing of plosives. In order to model realistic language change, speech sounds therefore have to be modelled in context.

Another reason why context is necessary is to allow agents to recognize words in which sounds have been modified. If in the vowel simulations a vowel changes position, it is learned as a different vowel by the other agents. However, in order for free variation, and therefore sound change, to occur, agents should be able to disambiguate a modified word. There should therefore be redundancy in the word, that is, extra information that renders it still recognizable. Such redundancy can in reality be provided by semantic context, but in the imitation game paradigm, such semantic context does not exist and the only way a word can be disambiguated is therefore by phonetic context.

How should such a system be implemented? Production and perception should be realistic models of the way humans produce and perceive speech sounds. For complex utterances it is also necessary that learning proceed in a more realistic way than in the vowel model, as many universals of complex sounds are probably caused in part by ease of learning. Finally, for a model of complex utterances to work, a reasonably realistic representation of speech sounds in the agents is necessary.

Production is probably the element that can be made the most realistic. Different articulatory models exist (Mermelstein 1973, Maeda 1989,

Boersma 1998). These are relatively uncontroversial, as they are based on physical measurements of the human vocal tract. Producing actual sounds with them is extremely calculation-intensive, so realism will have to be limited somewhat. An implementation of Mermelstein's (1973) model, but without a nasal cavity, has been made and this is shown in Figure 7.1.

Control of the different articulators is much more difficult. The muscles that control the different articulators are of course well known, but important parameters for simulating their movements, such as mass, stiffness, and elasticity, as well as the way in which the muscles are actually used in different utterances, are much less well known. Also, it is impossible to model the actions of all individual muscles in a simulation. In the preliminary implementation of a complex utterance agent, Saltzman's model, augmented with some of Browman and Goldstein's ideas (Saltzman 1986, Saltzman and Munhall 1989, Browman and Goldstein 1995), was used. It is based on simulating a damped mass–spring system moving towards a target. This model results in relatively realistic sound production.

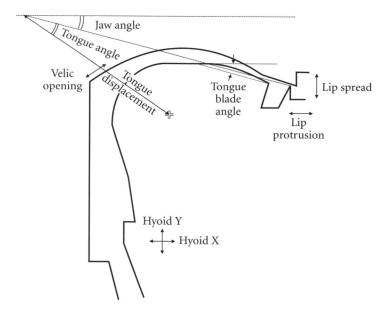

FIGURE 7.1. Mermelstein's articulatory model as implemented in the research into more complex utterances

Note: The model's control parameters are indicated.

Source: Mermelstein (1973).

Realistic perception is even more difficult. How a sound signal is analysed into its component frequencies in the inner ear is quite well known,
but it is much less clear exactly how the brain processes the neural signals
that are produced in the inner ear. It could well be that many idiosyncrasies
in the way humans perceive speech sounds arise in the neural processing
rather than in the ear itself. Models of the inner ear and the first layer
of neural processing do exist (Pont and Damper 1992), but these are
computationally complex. Fortunately, it is likely that a simple (weighted)
frequency analysis would produce interesting results. This would require
fewer computations.

Problems of production and perception are complex, but can in principle be resolved by physical measurements. More interesting are the problems of representation and learning of speech sounds. Trying to implement
the use and learning of complex speech sounds in a computer model can
help us to learn more about their nature. This is a third reason why doing
experiments with complex utterances is interesting.

Speech sounds can be analysed in terms of phonemes, the minimal units
of an utterance that can make a distinction in meaning. Although it is likely
that phonemes play a role in the way speech sounds are represented in
the brain, there are a number of problems with them that make it unlikely
that they are the only way of representing, or that speech sounds are
represented as phonemes exactly. First of all, phonemes cannot be isolated
from a speech signal in any straightforward way. In production too, speech
is not generated as a string of concatenated phonemes, but articulatory
gestures belonging to different phonemes are executed simultaneously.
This is due to co-articulation, but cannot be considered a purely physiological process. Under some circumstances, articulatory gestures influence
each other, while under other circumstances the same gestures do not
influence each other. In languages where rounding of front vowels is not
contrastive, for example, such as English, where [y] would be considered
an allophone of /i/, front vowels could become rounded in the context
of bilabial consonants. In languages where there is a contrast between
rounded and unrounded front vowels (such as French), such co-articulation is much less likely. There must therefore be a certain degree of
conscious control over articulatory actions that are smaller than phonemes.
Also, in languages that have large sets of complex consonants, such as !Xū
(Snyman 1970), the consonants form systems that could be analysed in
terms of sub-consonant gestures (see Table 7.1). As for larger utterances,

TABLE 7.1. The 48 clicks of the !Xū language

Dental

	Unasp.	Asp.	Nasalized		Velarized	
			Unasp.	Asp.		Glot.
Voiceless	ǀ	ǀʰ	ŋ̥ǀˀ	ŋǀʰ	ǀˠ	ŋ̥ǀˠˀ
Voiced	gǀ	gǀʰ	ŋǀ	ŋǀʰ	gǀˠ	gǀˠˀ

Alveolar

	Unasp.	Asp.	Nasalized		Velarized	
			Unasp.	Asp.		Glot.
Voiceless	ǃ	ǃʰ	ŋ̥ǃˀ	ŋǃʰ	ǃˠ	ŋ̥ǃˠˀ
Voiced	gǃ	gǃʰ	ŋǃ	ŋǃʰ	gǃˠ	gǃˠˀ

Palatal-alveolar

	Unasp.	Asp.	Nasalized		Velarized	
			Unasp.	Asp.		Glot.
Voiceless	ǂ	ǂʰ	ŋ̥ǂˀ	ŋǂʰ	ǂˠ	ŋ̥ǂˠˀ
Voiced	gǂ	gǂʰ	ŋǂ	ŋǂʰ	gǂˠ	gǂˠˀ

Alveolar-lateral

	Unasp.	Asp.	Nasalized		Velarized	
			Unasp.	Asp.		Glot.
Voiceless	ǁ	ǁʰ	ŋ̥ǁˀ	ŋǁʰ	ǁˠ	ŋ̥ǁˠˀ
Voiced	gǁ	gǁʰ	ŋǁ	ŋǁʰ	gǁˠ	gǁˠˀ

Note: The organization of the table is not meant to illustrate any phonological interpretation, but just to show that the system of clicks is very symmetrical, indicating that it is possible for different articulatory gestures to be used in combination. This indicates that there must be control and representation on a sub-phonemic level.
Source: Based on the work of Snyman (1970).

there seem to be occasions when speech sounds seem to behave as if they were organized in larger groups. Onsets of syllables often show regularities that are different from those of codas. Also, there are examples in which different phonemes in a word seem to influence each other, such as in vowel harmony (occurring in Turkish, for example) or nasal harmony. It appears that speech sounds are represented on different levels of detail in the human brain.

In a computer implementation a decision has to be made about how sounds are to be implemented. Of course, not all questions can be answered by a single computer simulation, so a compromise has to be found. Such a compromise has to be reasonably realistic and sufficiently flexible. In order to make a compromise, data from psycholinguistic research should be taken into account as well as phonological phenomena in different languages. It is probably necessary that the representation of sounds should change while the agent is learning. This illustrates that modelling is not only interesting for investigating universals, but could also shed light on the problem of how speech sounds might be implemented in the human brain.

In any case there have to be two levels of representation in the agent: a lexicon of words and a repertoire of sounds, even though at the beginning these might be quite similar. Words in humans are associated with meanings, but in the agents they will only serve as targets for imitation. There will be two steps in the analysis of a perceived signal: first it is analysed in terms of an agent's basic sounds, and then the resulting sequence of sounds is compared with the agent's words. The closest word is then considered to be recognized. In this way, words can be recognized and correctly imitated even if the sequences of sounds are not quite the same.

The last, and probably most difficult, question that has to be resolved is the one of how speech sounds are learned. A first implementation would probably be quite crude and use general prototype learning, such as is used in the vowel experiments, but it would have to solve a second problem of how to split up the words it hears into smaller, reusable units (whatever these units may be). Data from psycholinguistics, but especially on child acquisition of speech sounds, should be taken into account. Probably a progression from holistic storage of crude imitations of the sounds an agent uses to more analytic and precise storage is necessary. This would produce behaviour similar to that demonstrated by children learning a language. First they produce holistic utterances and then they seem to proceed to more analytic (phonemic) coding. Also, the level of detail they are capable of learning seems to increase; at first consonant clusters are reduced but they are produced with more and more accuracy during development (Vihman 1996). Another learning problem that has to be solved is how the inverse mapping, between perceived speech and articulations produced, takes place. Infants seem to be able to do this quite automatically, but it is not at all easy for a computer model. Given an acoustic signal, it is difficult to find the necessary articulatory actions to reproduce it. Perhaps babbling can serve as a means for learning how to map between perceived signals and articulatory actions, but it might also turn out that some of this mapping has to be innately specified.

In short, the modelling of complex utterances is necessary in order to make research into self-organization in speech sounds more interesting, but there are a large number of very difficult questions that have to be resolved first. However, work on resolving these questions has the potential for generating a large number of linguistically relevant results.

7.5 Relation between sounds and syntax

Although the human ability to use speech sounds in a combinatorial way is unique, the property of human language that is often considered to be most crucial is syntax. However, it may be that phonology and syntax share the same cognitive mechanisms and that the study of speech sounds could shed some light on the study of syntax as well.

In his book in this series, Carstairs-McCarthy (1999) develops a theory that links syntax and phonology. His theory is based on the observation of structural similarities between syllables and sentences. According to Carstairs-McCarthy, the fact that early humans started walking on two legs caused the larynx to descend. This opened up the possibility of a much larger repertoire of calls, which were organized as syllables. A tendency to avoid synonymy caused different meanings to be assigned to the different possible calls. The way in which simple calls were combined into longer structures (sentences) was adopted from the way sounds are structured into syllables.

Whether one is convinced by Carstairs-McCarthy's theory or not, it is clear that there are a number of similarities between phonology and syntax. Both are combinatorial: individual speech sounds can be combined into new words just as words and morphemes can be combined into new sentences. Both systems have rules that restrict the way in which the basic elements can be combined. Syntactical rules determine that morphemes and words cannot be combined in random sequences, just as phonotactical rules determine that speech sounds cannot be combined into random sequences. Finally, both systems have long-distance dependencies. In syntax, different words have to agree morphologically in categories such as gender and number throughout the sentence, while in phonology there are long-distance dependencies in such matters as vowel harmony and nasal harmony.

The main difference between syntactical structures and phonological structures is of course that in syntactical structures there is the possibility of recursion, whereas in phonological structures recursion is not allowed. Noun phrases can, for example, contain relative clauses that can again contain noun phrases. Syllables, on the other hand, have to consist of individual phonemes that do not consist of smaller elements, thus precluding the possibility of recursion.

The fact that there are similarities between phonology and syntax does not necessarily mean that they are linked in the brain. However, it does mean that if one tries to model phonology, one has to solve a number of important problems that one also has to solve if one wants to model syntax. In both cases temporal sequences have to be learned, something that is not necessary in models of lexicons, for example. In both syntax and phonology it is also necessary to extract smaller constituents from larger units. In phonology basic units of sound have to be extracted from utterances, while in syntax words and morphemes have to be extracted from sentences. This is a difficult learning problem, as the constituents are not generally used outside the larger units. It would therefore seem that any learning system that is able to learn phonology would also be able to learn a basic grammar (possibly one without recursion).

As phonetics and phonology are based on objectively measurable acoustic signals, the results of models in this field would be easier to compare with real human languages than would the results of models of syntax. Also, the study of speech sounds could make use of the fact that the way the brain handles speech can be investigated more easily than the way the brain handles syntactical structure. A study of how to model complex speech sounds could therefore open up the way for the study of syntax.

Perhaps more important for the study of language evolution is the fact that the similarities between the cognitive requirements for phonology and those for syntax indicate that it is unlikely that there has ever been a stage at which there was complex phonology (allowing compositionally made-up utterances) but no syntax. Speakers that have the cognitive capacities to analyse, learn, and produce complex utterances would use these same capacities to develop syntactical utterances through cultural evolution. It is much more likely that phonology and syntax have emerged in parallel and have influenced each other through (cultural) co-evolution and through partly using the same cognitive mechanisms.

In this light the study of self-organization in speech sounds through computer models is relevant not only for phonetics and phonology, but also, it turns out, for the study of other parts of language as well.

Bibliography

ADELMAN, G. (ed.) (1987) *Encyclopedia of Neuroscience*. Boston: Birkhäuser.

BALDWIN, J. MARK (1896) 'A new factor in evolution', *The American Naturalist*, 30, pp. 441–451, 536–553. Reprinted in R. K. Belew and M. Mitchell (eds) (1996) *Adaptive Individuals in Evolving Populations: Models and Algorithms*, SFI Studies in the Sciences of Complexity, Proc. Vol. XXVI. Reading, MA: Addison-Wesley.

BATALI, JOHN (1998) 'Computational simulations of the emergence of grammar'. In Hurford *et al.* (eds), pp. 405–426.

BERRAH, AHMED-RÉDA (1998) 'Évolution artificielle d'une société d'agents de parole: Un modèle pour l'émergence du code phonétique'. Thesis, Institut National Polytechnique de Grenoble, Spécialité Sciences Cognitives.

—— and RAFAEL LABOISSIÈRE (1999) 'SPECIES: An evolutionary model for the emergence of phonetic structures in an artificial society of speech agents'. In D. Floreano, J.-D. Nicoud, and F. Mondada (eds) *Advances in Artificial Life. Lecture Notes in Artificial Intelligence*, Vol. 1674, pp. 674–678. New York: Springer.

—— HERVÉ GLOTIN, RAFAEL LABOISSIÈRE, PIERRE BESSIÈRE, and LOUIS-JEAN BOË (1996) 'From form to formation of phonetic structures: An evolutionary computing perspective'. In Terry Fogarty and Gilles Venturini (eds) *ICML '96 Workshop on Evolutionary Computing and Machine Learning*, pp. 23–29. Bari.

BILLARD, A., and G. HAYES (1998) 'Transmitting communication skills through imitation in autonomous robots'. In A. Birk and J. Demiris (eds) *Learning Robots: A Multi-Perspective Exploration*, pp. 79–94. New York: Springer.

—— ——(1999) 'DRAMA: A connectionist architecture for control and learning in autonomous robots'. *Adaptive Behavior*, 7(1), pp. 35–64.

BOË, LOUIS-JEAN, JEAN-LUC SCHWARTZ, and NATHALIE VALLÉE (1995) 'The prediction of vowel systems: Perceptual contrast and stability'. In Eric Keller (ed.) *Fundamentals of Speech Synthesis and Speech Recognition*, pp. 185–213. Chichester: John Wiley.

BOERSMA, PAUL (1998) *Functional Phonology*. The Hague: Holland Academic Graphics.

BRISCOE, TED (in press) *Linguistic Evolution through Language Acquisition: Formal and Computational Models*. Cambridge: Cambridge University Press.

BROOKS, R. (1990) 'Elephants don't play chess', *Robotics and Autonomous Systems*, 6, pp. 3–15.

—— (1991) 'Intelligence without representation', *Artificial Intelligence*, 47, pp. 139–159.

BROWMAN, CATHERINE P., and LOUIS GOLDSTEIN (1995) 'Dynamics and articulatory phonology'. In Robert F. Port and Timothy van Gelder (eds) *Mind as Motion*, pp. 175–194. Cambridge, MA: MIT Press.

BUHR, R. (1980) 'The emergence of vowels in an infant', *Journal of Speech and Hearing Research*, 23, pp. 73–94.

CALVIN, W. H., and D. BICKERTON (2000) *Lingua ex Machina: Reconciling Darwin and Chomsky with the Human Brain*. Cambridge, MA: MIT Press.

CARLSON, R., B. GRANSTRÖM, and G. FANT (1970) 'Some studies concerning perception of isolated vowels', *STL/QPSR* (Speech Transmission Laboratory Quarterly Progress and Status Report, Department of Speech Communication and Music Acoustics, KTH, Stockholm), 2/3, pp. 19–35.

CARRÉ, RENÉ (1994) ' "Speaker" and "speech" characteristics: A deductive approach', *Phonetica*, 51, pp. 7–16.

—— (1996) 'Prediction of vowel systems using a deductive approach', *Proceedings of the ICSLP 96*, pp. 434–437. Philadelphia.

—— and MOHAMAD MRAYATI (1995) 'Vowel transitions, vowel systems, and the Distinctive Region Model'. In C. Sorin *et al.* (eds) *Levels in Speech Communication: Relations and Interactions*, pp. 73–89. Amsterdam: Elsevier.

CARSTAIRS-MCCARTHY, A. (1999) *The Origins of Complex Language: An Inquiry into the Evolutionary Beginnings of Sentences, Syllables, and Truth*. Oxford: Oxford University Press.

CHOI, V. D. (1991) 'Kabardian vowels revisited', *Journal of the International Phonetic Association*, 21, pp. 4–12.

CHOMSKY, NOAM (1965) *Aspects of the Theory of Syntax*. Cambridge, MA: MIT Press.

—— (1972) *Language and Mind*, enlarged edition. New York: Harcourt Brace Jovanovich.

—— (1975) *Reflections on Language*. New York: Pantheon Books.

—— (1980) 'Rules and representations', *The Behavioural and Brain Sciences*, 3, pp. 1–21.

—— and MORRIS HALLE (1968) *The Sound Pattern of English*. Cambridge, MA: MIT Press.

COMRIE, BERNARD (1981) *Language Typology and Linguistic Universals*. Oxford: Blackwell

COOPER, FRANKLIN S., PIERRE C. DELATTRE, ALVIN M. LIBERMAN, JOHN M. BORST, and LOUIS J. GERSTMAN (1976) 'Some experiments on the perception of synthetic speech sounds'. In D. B. Fry (ed.) *Acoustic Phonetics*, pp. 258–283. Cambridge: Cambridge University Press.

CROTHERS, JOHN (1978) 'Typology and universals of vowel systems'. In Joseph H. Greenberg, Charles A. Ferguson, and Edith A. Moravcsik (eds) *Universals of Human Language*, Vol. 2, *Phonology*, pp. 93–152. Stanford: Stanford University Press.

DARWIN, CHARLES (1859) *On the Origin of Species.* Reprinted: Harmondsworth: Penguin Classics, 1985.

DAWKINS, RICHARD (1976) *The Selfish Gene.* Oxford: Oxford University Press.

DE BOER, BART G. (1999) 'Self-organisation in vowel systems'. Ph.D. Thesis, Vrije Universiteit Brussel.

——— (2000) 'Emergence of vowel systems through self-organisation', *AI Communications*, 13, pp. 27–39.

——— (in press) 'Self-organisation in vowel systems', *Journal of Phonetics*, 2, pp. 441–465.

DE JONG, EDWIN D. (1998) 'The development of a lexicon based on behavior'. In Han La Poutré and Jaap van den Herik (eds) *Proceedings of the Xth Netherlands/ Belgium Conference on Artificial Intelligence, Amsterdam, 18–19 November 1998*, pp. 27–36.

——— (1999) 'Autonomous concept formation'. In T. Dean (ed.) *Proceedings of the Sixteenth International Joint Conference on Artificial Intelligence IJCAI '99*, pp. 344–349. San Francisco, CA: Morgan Kaufmann.

DE LAMARCK, J. B. (1809) *Philosophie zoologique: Ou exposition des considérations relatives à l'histoire naturelle des animaux.* Paris.

DERBYSHIRE, D. C., and G. K. PULLUM (1981) 'Object initial languages', *International Journal of American Linguistics*, 47(3), pp. 192–214.

DE SAUSSURE, FERDINAND (1987) *Cours de linguistique générale: Édition préparée par Tullio de Mauro*, Paris: Payot.

DIXON, R. M. W. (1972) *The Dyirbal Language of North Queensland*, Cambridge Studies in Linguistics, 9. Cambridge: Cambridge University Press.

——— (1997) *The Rise and Fall of Languages.* Cambridge: Cambridge University Press.

EVERETT, DANIEL L. (1982) 'Phonetic rarities in Piraha', *Journal of the International Phonetic Association*, 12/2, pp. 94–96.

FIRCHOW, IWIN, and JACQUELINE FIRCHOW (1969) 'An abbreviated phoneme inventory', *Anthropological Linguistics*, 11, pp. 271–276.

FRIEDA, E. M., A. C. WALLEY, J. E. FLEGE, and M. E. SLOANE (1999) 'Adults' perception of native and nonnative vowels: Implications for the perceptual magnet effect', *Perception & Psychophysics*, 61(3), pp. 561–577.

GASSER, MICHAEL (ed.) (1998) *The Grounding of Word Meaning: Data and Models, Papers from the 1998 Workshop.* Menlo Park, CA: AAAI Press.

GLOTIN, HERVÉ (1995) 'La Vie artificielle d'une société de robots parlants: Émergence et changement du code phonétique'. DEA thesis, Institut National Polytechnique de Grenoble.

——— and RAFAEL LABOISSIÈRE (1996) 'Emergence du code phonétique dans une société de robots parlants', *Actes de la Conférence de Rochebrune 1996: Du Collectif au Social.* Paris: Ecole Nationale Supérieure des Télécommunications.

GOLDBERG, DAVID E. (1998) *Genetic Algorithms in Search, Optimization, and Machine Learning.* Reading, MA: Addison-Wesley.

GOULD, S. J. (1991) *The Flamingo's Smile*. London: Penguin Books.

GREENBERG, J. H. (1966) 'Some universals of grammar with particular reference to order of meaningful elements'. In J. H. Greenberg (ed.) *Universals of Language*, 2nd edition. Cambridge, MA: MIT Press.

GRIESER, D., and P. K. KUHL (1989) 'Categorization of speech by infants: Support for speech-sound prototypes', *Developmental Psychology*, 25(4), pp. 577–588.

GRIMES, BARBARA F. (ed.) (1996) *Ethnologue: Languages of the World*, 13th edition. Dallas: Summer Institute of Linguistics.

HASHIMOTO, M. J. (1973) *The Hakka Dialect: A Linguistic Study of Phonology, Syntax and Lexicon*. Cambridge: Cambridge University Press.

HASSELBRINK, G. (1965) *Alternative Analyses of the Phonemic System in Central South-Lappish*. The Hague: Bloomington.

HAUSER, MARC D. (1997) *The Evolution of Communication*. Cambridge, MA: MIT Press.

HOCK, H. H. (1991) *Principles of Historical Linguistics*, 2nd edition. Berlin: Mouton de Gruyter.

HOCKETT, C. F. (1955) *A Manual of Phonology*. Baltimore: Waverly Press.

HOPPER, P. J., and E. C. TRAUGOTT (1993) *Grammaticalization*. Cambridge: Cambridge University Press.

HURFORD, JAMES R. (1987) *Language and Number*. Oxford: Blackwell.

—— (2000) 'Social transmission favours linguistic generalization'. In Studdert-Kennedy *et al.* (eds).

—— MICHAEL STUDDERT-KENNEDY, and CHRIS KNIGHT (eds) (1998) *Approaches to the Evolution of Language* (selected papers from the 2nd International Conference on the Evolution of Language, London, 6–9 April 1998). Cambridge: Cambridge University Press.

JAKOBSON, ROMAN, and MORRIS HALLE (1956) *Fundamentals of Language*. The Hague: Mouton.

JESPERSEN, OTTO (1968) *Language, its Nature, Development and Origin*. London: Allen and Unwin.

JUSCZYK, PETER W. (1997) *The Discovery of Spoken Language*. Cambridge, MA: MIT Press.

KAPLAN, F. (1998) 'Rôle de la simulation multi-agent pour comprendre l'origine et l'évolution du langage'. In J.-P. Barthès, V. Chevrier, and C. Brassac (eds) *Système multi-agents: De l'interaction à la socialité* (JFIADSMA98), pp. 51–64. Paris: Hermès.

KIRBY, SIMON (1998) 'Fitness and the selective adaptation of language'. In Hurford *et al.* (eds) pp. 359–383.

—— (1999) *Function, Selection, and Innateness: The Emergence of Language Universals*. Oxford: Oxford University Press.

—— and JAMES R. HURFORD (1997) 'Learning, culture and evolution in the origin of linguistic constraints'. In Phil Husbands and Inman Harvey (eds) *Fourth European Conference on Artificial Life*, pp. 493–502. Cambridge, MA: MIT Press.

KITANO, H., M. ASADA, Y. KUNIYOSHI, I. NODA, and E. OSAWA (1997) 'Robocup: The robot world cup initiative'. In *Proceedings of the First International Conference on Autonomous Agents*, pp. 340–347. New York: The ACM Press.

KUHL, P. K., and A. N. MELTZOFF (1996) 'Infant vocalization in response to speech: Vocal imitation and developmental change', *Journal of the Acoustical Society of America*, 100(4), pp. 2425–2438.

—— K. A. WILLIAMS, F. LACERDA, K. N. STEVENS, and B. LINDBLOM (1992) 'Linguistic experience alters phonetic perception in infants by 6 months of age', *Science*, 255, pp. 606–608.

—— J. E., ANDRUSKI, I. A. CHISTOVICH, L. A. CHISTOVICH, E. V. KOZHEVIKOVA, V. L. RYSINKA, E. I. STOLYAROVA, U. SUNDBERG, and F. LACERDA (1997) 'Cross-language analysis of phonetic units in language addressed to infants', *Science*, 277, pp. 684–686.

LABOV, W. (1994) *Principles of Linguistic Change: Internal Factors*. Oxford: Blackwell.

LADEFOGED, PETER, and IAN MADDIESON (1996) *The Sounds of the World's Languages*. Oxford: Blackwell.

LAKOFF, G. (1987) *Women, Fire, and Dangerous Things: What Categories Reveal about the Mind*. Chicago: Chicago University Press.

LANGTON, CHRISTOPHER G. (ed.) (1989) *Artificial Life*. Reading, MA: Addison-Wesley.

—— CHARLES TAYLOR, J. DOYNE FARMER, and STEEN RASMUSSEN (eds) (1990) *Artificial Life II*. Reading, MA: Addison-Wesley.

LAVER, J. (1994) *Principles of Phonetics*. Cambridge: Cambridge University Press.

LIBERMAN, ALVIN M., PIERRE C. DELATTRE, FRANKLIN S. COOPER, and LOUIS J. GERSTMAN (1976) 'The role of consonant–vowel transitions in the perception of the stop and nasal consonants'. In D. B. Fry (ed.) *Acoustic Phonetics*. Cambridge: Cambridge University Press.

LILJENCRANTS, L., and BJÖRN LINDBLOM (1972) 'Numerical simulations of vowel quality systems: The role of perceptual contrast', *Language*, 48, pp. 839–862.

LINDBLOM, BJÖRN (1972) 'Phonetics and the description of language'. In André Rigault and René Charbonneau (eds) *Proceedings of the Seventh International Congress on Phonetic Sciences*, pp. 63–93. The Hague: Mouton.

—— (1986) 'Phonetic universals in vowel systems'. In J. J. Ohala and J. J. Jaeger (eds) *Experimental Phonology*, pp. 13–44. Orlando, FL: Academic Press.

—— (unpublished) 'From second thoughts to first principles'.

—— and JAMES LUBKER (1985) 'The speech homunculus and a problem of phonetic linguistics'. In Victoria A. Fromkin (ed.) *Phonetic Linguistics: Essays in Honor of Peter Ladefoged*, pp. 169–192. Orlando: Academic Press.

—— and OLLE ENGSTRAND (1989) 'In what sense is speech quantal?' *Journal of Phonetics*, 17, pp. 107–121.

—— and IAN MADDIESON (1988) 'Phonetic universals in consonant systems'. In Larry M. Hyman and Charles N. Li (eds) *Language, Speech and Mind*, pp. 62–78. London: Routledge.

LINDBLOM, BJÖRN, PETER MACNEILAGE, and MICHAEL STUDDERT-KENNEDY (1984) 'Self-organizing processes and the explanation of language universals'. In Brian Butterworth, Bernard Comrie, and Östen Dahl (eds) *Explanations for Language Universals*, pp. 181–203. Berlin: Walter de Gruyter & Co.

LIVINGSTONE, D., and C. FYFE (1999) 'Modelling the evolution of linguistic diversity'. In D. Floreano, J.-D. Nicoud, and F. Mondada (eds) *Advances in Artificial Life. Lecture Notes in Artificial Intelligence*, Vol. 1674, pp. 704–708. Berlin: Springer.

MADDIESON, IAN (1978) 'Universals of tone'. In Joseph H. Greenberg, Charles A. Ferguson, and Edith A. Moravcsik (eds) *Universals of Human Language*, Vol. 2, *Phonology*, pp. 335–365. Stanford: Stanford University Press.

—— (1984) *Patterns of Sounds*. Cambridge: Cambridge University Press.

—— and KRISTIN PRECODA (1990) 'Updating UPSID', *UCLA Working Papers in Phonetics*, 74, pp. 104–111.

MAEDA, SHINJI (1989) 'Compensatory articulation during speech: Evidence from the analysis and synthesis of vocal tract shapes using an articulatory model'. In W. J. Hardcastle and A. Marchal (eds) *Speech Production and Speech Modelling*, pp. 131–149. Dordrecht: Kluwer.

MANTAKAS, M., J. L. SCHWARTZ, and P. ESCUDIER (1986) 'Modèle de prédiction du "deuxième formant effectif" F_2'—application à l'étude de la labialité des voyelles avant du français'. In *Proceedings of the 15th Journées d'Étude sur la Parole*, pp. 157–161. Paris: Société Française d'Acoustique.

MAYNARD SMITH, J., and E. SZATHMARY (1997) *The Major Transitions in Evolution*. Oxford: Oxford University Press.

MERMELSTEIN, P. (1973) 'Articulatory model for the study of speech production', *Journal of the Acoustical Society of America*, 53(4), pp. 1070–1082.

NETTLE, D. (1999) *Linguistic Diversity*. Oxford: Oxford University Press.

NICHOLS, J. (1992) *Linguistic Diversity in Space and Time*. Chicago: University of Chicago Press.

NICOLIS, G., and I. PRIGOGINE (1977) *Self-Organization in Non-Equilibrium Systems*. New York: John Wiley.

OLIPHANT, M. (1993) 'Conditions for the evolution of saussurean communication'. Master's thesis, University of California, San Diego.

—— (1996) 'The dilemma of saussurean communication', *Biosystems*, 37(1–2), pp. 31–38.

—— (1999) 'The learning barrier: Moving from innate to learned systems of communication', *Adaptive Behavior*, 7(3–4), pp. 371–384.

PETERSON, G. E., and H. L. BARNEY (1952) 'Control methods used in a study of the vowels', *Journal of the Acoustical Society of America*, 24(2), pp. 175–184.

PETITOT-COCORDA, J. (1985) *Les Catastrophes de la parole*. Paris: Maloine.

PONT, M. J., and R. I. DAMPER (1992) 'A computational model of afferent neural activity from the cochlea to the dorsal acoustic stria', *Journal of the Acoustical Society of America*, 89, pp. 1213–1228.

PRIGOGINE, I., and I. STENGERS (1988) *Order out of Chaos: Man's New Dialogue with Nature.* London: Fontana Paperbacks.

RABINER, L. R., and R. W. SCHAFER (1978) *Digital Processing of Speech Signals.* Englewood Cliffs, NJ: Prentice-Hall.

ROBERT-RIBES, J. (1995) 'Modèles d'intégration audiovisuelle de signaux linguistiques: De la perception humaine à la reconnaissance automatique des voyelles'. Ph.D. thesis, Institut National Polytechnique de Grenoble.

ROUSSEAU, JEAN-JACQUES (1986) 'Essay on the origin of languages which treats of melody and musical imitation'. In John H. Moran and Alexander Gode (eds) *On the Origin of Language*, pp. 1–74. Chicago: Chicago University Press.

ROUX J.-C., R. H. SIMOYI, and H. L. SWINNEY (1983) 'Observation of a strange attractor', *Physica D*, 8, pp. 257–266.

SALTZMAN, ELLIOT L. (1986) 'Task dynamic coordination of the speech articulators', *Experimental Brain Research Series*, 15, pp. 129–144.

—— and KEVIN G. MUNHALL (1989) 'A dynamical approach to patterning in speech production', *Ecological Psychology*, 1(4), pp. 333–382.

SCHWARTZ, JEAN-LUC, LOUIS-JEAN BOË, NATHALIE VALLÉE, and CHRISTIAN ABRY (1997*a*) 'Major trends in vowel system inventories', *Journal of Phonetics*, 25, pp. 233–253.

————————(1997*b*) 'The dispersion–focalization theory of vowel systems', *Journal of Phonetics*, 25, pp. 255–286.

SEDLAK, P. (1969) 'Typological considerations of vowel quality systems', *Working Papers on Language Universals*, 1, pp. 1–40. Stanford, CA: Stanford University Press.

SEIDEN, W. (1960) 'Chamorro phonemes', *Anthropological Linguistics*, 2(4), pp. 6–33.

SHELDON, S. N. (1974) 'Some morphophonemic and tone rules in Mura-Pirahã', *International Journal of American Linguistics*, 40, pp. 279–282.

SNYMAN, J. W. (1970) *An Introduction to the !Xũ (!Kung) Language.* Cape Town: Balkema.

STARK, R. E. (1980) 'Stages of speech development in the first year of life', In G. Yenikomshian, J. F. Kavanagh, and C. A. Ferguson (eds) *Child Phonology 1: Production.* New York: Academic Press.

STEELS, LUC (1995) 'A self-organizing spatial vocabulary', *Artificial Life*, 2(3), pp. 319–332.

—— (1997*a*) 'Constructing and sharing perceptual distinctions'. In Maarten van Someren and G. Widmer (eds) *Proceedings of the ECML.* Berlin: Springer.

—— (1997*b*) 'The synthetic modelling of language origins', *Evolution of Communication,* 1(1), pp. 1–34.

—— (1997*c*) 'Language learning and language contact'. In W. Daelemans (ed.) *Proceedings of the Workshop on Empirical Approaches to Language Acquisition.* Prague.

—— (1998*a*) 'Synthesising the origins of language and meaning using co-evolution, self-organisation and level formation'. In Hurford *et al.* (eds), pp. 384–404.

STEELS, LUC (1998*b*) 'The origins of syntax in visually grounded robotic agents', *Artificial Intelligence*, 103, pp. 1–24.

—— (1999) 'The spontaneous self-organization of an adaptive language'. In K. Furukawa, D. Michie, and S. Muggleton (eds) *Machine Intelligence*, 15: *Intelligent Agents*, ch. 11. Oxford: Oxford University Press.

—— and FRÉDÉRIC KAPLAN (1997) 'Spontaneous lexicon change. Stochasticity as a source of innovation in language games'. In C. Adami, R. Belew, H. Kitano, and C. Taylor (eds) *Proceedings of Artificial Life VI*, pp. 368–376. Cambridge, MA: MIT Press.

—— and ANGUS MCINTYRE (1999) 'Spatially distributed naming games', *Advances in Complex Systems*, 1(4), pp. 301–324.

—— and PAUL VOGT (1997) 'Grounding adaptive language games in robotic agents'. In Phil Husbands and Inman Harvey (eds) *Proceedings of the Fourth European Conference on Artificial Life*, pp. 474–482. Cambridge, MA: MIT Press.

STEVENS, KENNETH N. (1972) 'The quantal nature of speech: Evidence from articulatory-acoustic data'. In E. E. David, Jr., and P. B. Denes (eds) *Human Communication: A Unified View*, pp. 51–66. New York: McGraw-Hill.

—— (1989) 'On the quantal nature of speech', *Journal of Phonetics* 17(1), pp. 3–45.

STUDDERT-KENNEDY, M., J. R. HURFORD, and C. KNIGHT (eds) (2000) *The Evolutionary Emergence of Language: Social Function and the Origins of Linguistic Form*. Cambridge: Cambridge University Press.

SUZUKI, JUNJI, and KUNIHIKO KANEKO (1994) 'Imitation games', *Physica D*, 75, pp. 325–342.

TAATGEN, N. A., and J. R. ANDERSON (unpublished) 'Why do children learn to say "broke"?'

TRUBETZKOY, N. S. (1929) 'Zur allgemeinen Theorie der phonologischen Vokalsysteme', *Travaux du Cercle Linguistique de Prague*, 7, pp. 39–67.

TURING, ALAN M. (1950) 'Computing machinery and intelligence', *Mind*, 59, pp. 433–460.

VALLÉE, NATHALIE (1994) 'Systèmes vocaliques: De la typologie aux prédictions'. Thesis, Institut de la Communication Parlée (Grenoble-URA C.N.R.S. no 368).

VAN LOOVEREN, J. (1999) 'Multiple word naming games'. In E. Postma and M. Gyssens (eds) *Proceedings of BNAIC '99*, pp. 195–202

—— (2000) 'Analysis of multiple word naming games'. Accepted for BNAIC 2000.

VANVIK, A. (1972) 'A phonetic-phonemic analysis of Standard Eastern Norwegian', *Norwegian Journal of Linguistics*, 26, pp. 119–164.

VENNEMANN, THEO (1988) *Preference Laws for Syllable Structure*. Berlin: Mouton de Gruyter.

VIHMAN, M. (ed) (1976) *A Reference Manual and User's Guide for the Stanford Phonology Archive*, part 1. Stanford, CA: Stanford University Press.

VIHMAN, MARILYN MAY (1996) *Phonological Development: The Origins of Language in the Child*. Cambridge, MA: Blackwell.

VOGT, PAUL (2000) 'Grounding language about actions: Mobile robots playing follow me games'. In J. A. Meyer, A. Bertholz, D. Floreano, H. Roitblat, and S. Wilson (eds) *SAB 2000 Proceedings. Supplement Book*. Paris: International Society for Adaptive Behavior.

WERNER, G., and M. DYER (1991) 'Evolution of communication in artificial organisms'. In C. Langton, C. Taylor, J. Framer, and S. Rasmussen (eds) *Artificial life II*, pp. 659–687. Redwood City, CA: Addison-Wesley.

WILDGEN, W. (1990) 'Basic principles of self-organisation in language'. In H. Haken and M. Stadler (eds) *Synergetics of Cognition*, pp. 415–426. Berlin: Springer.

WITTGENSTEIN, L. (1967) *Philosophische Untersuchungen*. Frankfurt: Suhrkamp.

Index